THE GREAT
IRON HORSE
CHASE:
EUROPE

Published by

MELROSE BOOKS

An Imprint of Melrose Press Limited
St Thomas Place, Ely
Cambridgeshire
CB7 4GG, UK
www.melrosebooks.com

FIRST EDITION

Cover designed by Matt Stephens

ISBN 978 1 906561 83 3

Printed and bound in Great Britain by:
CPI Antony Rowe, Chippenham, Wiltshire

Dedication

I would like to dedicate this book to my wife Joan and daughter Victoria. Since I opted for retirement, they both have had to suffer me 'being around' to a far greater extent. Their support, suggestions and criticisms have, however, resulted in, I hope, a far better publication than might have been. Also to my parents who, unwittingly, set me on a career path on the railways which sparked a lifetime's love of the Iron Horse.

Acknowledgements

I would like to acknowledge the book being proofread by Paul Howard – a lifelong friend of both Bill and me. His checking of the accuracy of, in particular, the steam locomotive specifications/wheel arrangements etc., was most appreciated.

And to all the staff at Melrose Books who have guided/led/helped a new author through the process leading to this publication.

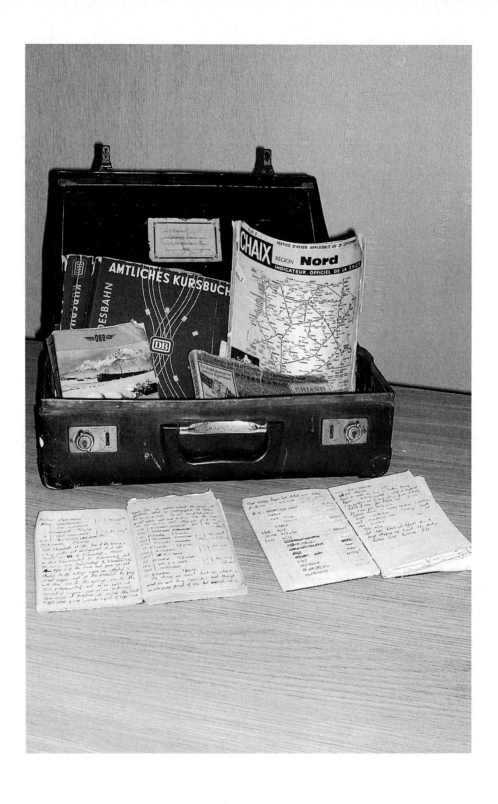

I T WAS 1962 WHEN I FIRST MET Bill when we both worked at the Divisional Manager's Office (South Western Division) offices of the Southern Region – then located at Waterloo. It was in the Fares and Excursions office, which was located 'in the gods' on the 4th floor, that he was forever arriving with boxes of photographs depicting steam trains and line closures. He was always saying "use your travel facilities and get out there – it's all disappearing!" and eventually – regrettably not until 1963 – I started what became an addiction: my steam travels. Whilst his interest in British steam tapered off in the mid-Sixties, moving on to Europe, mine dramatically increased from touring Britain right through till the end – in 1968. I had moved jobs in 1966 to the Divisional Manager's Office (South Eastern Division) near Cannon Street before eventually meeting up with Bill again when returning to the SWD – albeit now at Wimbledon. With the reduction of British steam, Bill again came to the rescue by suggesting that Europe had a lot to offer. The results of those 13 months, from the February of '68 to March '69 during which I made several week-long trips with him, form the major part of this book. His continued interest in World Steam and my 'disappearance' into domesticity meant that our paths did not cross again until 1990 when he organised a well attended 25th anniversary get-together in a pub at Wimbledon. Having, over the last few years, had some articles published in the British railway press about my travels throughout Britain in the Sixties, I attempted to 'sell' a couple of European equivalents – without success. I thought no more of it until, courtesy of *Steam Days* editor Rex Kennedy, Bill contacted me by email in 2007. We arranged to meet at Croydon where it was agreed that joint effort be put into a book for which, if I wrote the story, he would supply the photographs. I was on the point of contacting Bill, with the information that I had completed a 27,000 word document to which he was to attach accompanying photographs and proofread, when the devastating news came through that he had passed away. If I succeed in getting this tome published, with or without Bill's photographs, I would like it to be regarded as a fitting epitaph to him for two reasons. Firstly, for services rendered to the railway press (his photographs appearing in many publications) and, secondly, for instigating in me a lifelong interest in – addiction to, even – the steam locomotive. Rest in peace, Bill.

Keith Widdowson

GREAT IRON HORSE CHASE

CONTENTS
& LIST OF FIGURES

BILL SUMNER   V

INTRODUCTION   XI

CHAPTER ONE   THE OLYMPIC HOPES   1

CHAPTER TWO   ITALIAN AFFAIRS   7

2.01 – 880.054 at Chignolo Po with the 13:32 Pavia to Mantova on Monday 19/02/68.

2.02 – 625.156 arrived at Bassano Del Grappa with the 13:09 from Padova on Tuesday 20/02/68 – with Bill in the shot!

2.03 – 685.222 being attached at Cremona to the rear of the 15:45 Mantova to Cadogna. 19/02/68.

CHAPTER THREE   AUSTRIAN ADVENTURES   16

3.01 – Mistelbach shed on Wednesday 21/02/68.

3.02 – 93.1360 arriving at Prinzendorf Rannersdorf with the 11 05 Hohenau to Mistelbach on 21/02/68.

3.03 – 52.3688 at Leoben with the 12 10 to Eisenerz on 22/02/68.

3.04 – 97.209 at Prabichl with the 12 10 Leoben to Eisenerz on 22/02/68.

3.05 – The view from the Gasthof at Selzthal on Friday 23/02/68.

3.06 – 09:40 Selzthal to Bruck, Friday 23/02/68

CHAPTER FOUR   ONE OF CHAUMONT'S FINEST   30

CHAPTER FIVE   THE BASTILLE 'STORMING'   33

5.01 – 231G81 coming off the *Golden Arrow* at Amiens on Friday 15/03/68.

5.02 – 141TB457 (09:00) & 141TB477 (10:00) at Paris Bastille with departures for Boissey St Leger on Saturday 16/03/68.

5.03 – 241P26 at Chaumont with the 12:25 Paris Est to Basle/Berne on Saturday 16/03/68.

CHAPTER SIX   THE FIRST GERMAN INVASION   39

6.01 – 03.251 departing Monchengladbach with a 'footex' on Saturday 18/05/68.

6.02 – 01.008 arriving at Euskirchen with the 11:35 Saarbrucken to Emden on Saturday 18/05/68.

CHAPTER SEVEN   STUTTGART 604: A STEAM AGE RAIL ROVER   44

7.01 – 65.002 at Furth with the 06:06 from Weinheim on Thursday 30/05/68.

7.02 – 023.062-3 arriving at Bad FJ with the 11:48 Stuttgart to Heidelberg on Thursday. 30/05/68.

7.03 – Crailsheim on Friday 31/05/68 sees 038.499-0 on the 14:19 to Heilbronn and 50.1028 & 78.355 on the 14:30 to Aalen.

7.04 – 23.105 (the last steam locomotive built for DB) is seen at Crailsheim whilst working the 09:21 Ulm to Lauda on Saturday 01/06/68.

7.05 – 50.227 & 038.095-6 at Sinsheim with the 12:46 Heidelberg to Heilbronn on Monday 03/06/68.

7.06 – 78.355 at Aalen with the 16:07 to Crailsheim on Friday 31/05/68.

CHAPTER EIGHT   THE HIGHS AND LOWS OF A FRENCH TANK HUNT   58

8.01 – 242TA 105 at Croix Wasquehal (Northern France) on 29/06/68.

8.02 – At Gannet 141R1108 takes over the 22:16 Bordeaux to Geneve on Sunday 30/06/68.

8.03 – 141F189 on shed at Ussel on Sunday 30/06/68.

8.04 – Stored unserviceable at Ussel on Sunday 30/06/68 are 141TAs 310, 347, 336, 441, 332 and 486.

8.05 – 242TA102 at Lille with the 07:30 Paris Nord to Tourcoing on Saturday 29/06/68.

CHAPTER NINE   GO WEST, YOUNG MAN   66

9.01 – 141P150 at Paris Montparnasse with the 08:00 to Granville on Saturday 31/08/68.

9.02 – 141C181 having arrived at Savanay on Monday 02/09/68.

9.03 – 231D589 on shed at Le Croisic – Monday 02/09/68.

9.04 – 141R5587 readies herself for departure from Boulogne Maritime with the 13:18 Relief to Paris Nord on Friday 30/08/68.

CHAPTER TEN   FROM THE LAKES TO THE FORESTS AND BACK   74

10.01 – 86.419 at Rodach with the 17:26 from Coburg on Friday 06/09/68.

10.02 – 01.202 at Munchberg with the 11:26 Lichtenfels to Hof on Friday 06/09/68.

10.03 – 03.222 at Bregenz (Austria) on Sunday 08/09/68.

10.04 – 38.1282 at Tuttlingen with the 11:12 to Stuttgart on Wednesday 04/09/68.

10.05 – 03.222 at At Lustenau (Austria) on Sunday 08/09/68.

CHAPTER ELEVEN   THE PACIFIC DELUGE   87

11.01 – 231K8 prepares to work the 14:14 *Golden Arrow* out of Calais Maritime for Paris Nord on Saturday 19/10/68.

CHAPTER TWELVE   MORE TANKS – BUT NO MORE MOUNTAINS!   90

12.01 – Paris Nord and 141TCs 4 and 34 awaiting departure on Friday 08/11/68.

CHAPTER THIRTEEN   NEARLY THERE   94

CHAPTER FOURTEEN   LAST RITES OF THE *ARROW*   96

CHAPTER FIFTEEN   ITALY REVISITED   98

15.01 – 640.121 at Alba with an all stations locale on 21/02/69.

CHAPTER SIXTEEN   AN ARRESTING EXPERIENCE   104

16.01 – 06.006 at Spielfeld Strass (Yugo/Austrian border) on 26/02/69.

16.02 – 06.021 at Zagreb with the 08 00 to Maribor on 26/02/69.

CHAPTER SEVENTEEN AUSTRIA REVISITED   110

Chapter Eighteen   Across the Borders   115
  18.01 – 50.2838 at Dogern (Southern Germany) on 01/03/69.

Chapter Nineteen   Mad as a March Hare   118

Chapter Twenty   That's All, Folks   119

Appendix I   Train 1109 – 18. 57 Paris (Lyon) to
                    Clermont Ferrand – Friday 30TH August 1968   121

Appendix II   Index of Steam Runs   130

INTRODUCTION | XI

As, AT THE TIME I AM WRITING this book, the journeys undertaken were all over 40 years ago, if I were to rely on memories and photographs alone of the 'expeditions' undertaken during 1968/9 then the details could only have been guessed at. It was therefore most fortuitous that the small four by six inch red notebooks which accompanied me throughout my European exploits have survived life's many subsequent domestic turbulences. In them I had meticulously noted not only the trains/locomotives travelled on/with but also any accompanying minutiae without which a book such as this would be merely comprised of a monotonous list of journeys made (see appendix II). My quest for a lifetime's ambition of runs behind 1,000 steam locomotives appeared doomed because, by early 1968, there were just a handful of trains operated by steam power remaining in Britain. The suggestion from my friend Bill, the catalyst for my original addiction to steam in 1964 (hasn't he a lot to answer for?), that I try the European scene started me off on a 13 month European voyage of discovery. The resurrection of interest in chasing steam locomotives was reignited and by visiting France, Italy, Austria, West Germany and Yugoslavia, during which I accumulated 9,580 miles with 266 locomotives from 36 classes, I finally achieved, in the February of '69, the ultimate high point of my 1,000th steam locomotive. This is not, therefore, a comprehensive list of what steam was available throughout Europe during those years – that would equate to a far larger publication. This is my personal diary – with some accompanying photographs from Bill, my travelling mentor – of where I went during those 13 hectic months. I hope it both entertains and informs readers of a scenario long since disappeared.

To set the scene away from railways, in January of 1968 Czechoslovakia had democratically elected Alexander Dubcek as its new president. His policies, however, were far too liberal for the USSR's liking and 200,000 Warsaw pact troops 'retook' the country in the August. Throughout the year, worldwide protests were held against America's role in the Vietnam War whilst, in France, student riots and strikes, which were to severely affect my own travels, were held in protest against General de Gaulle's government – finally causing him to step down in the Spring of '69.

Closer to home, in March the Foreign Secretary, George Brown, resigned over the currency crisis which resulted in the devaluing of the pound; to be followed, the next month, by Enoch Powell's infamous *Rivers of Blood* speech, warning against the immigration and anti-discrimination legislation being processed through Parliament. Tony Hancock died in the June; Alec Rose completed his circumnavigation of the world the following month; and finally, in November, the Beatles issued their untitled *White Album*. The first decimal coins were issued: in 1968 the five and ten pence, and in 1969, the 50 pence, in readiness for the complete changeover in 1971.

And, finally, pirate radio ships. In the early Sixties, pop music was not played regularly on the BBC and with no commercial radio stations, the Light Programme (forerunner of Radio 2) preferred the likes of Acker Bilk and Vera Lynn. The only outlets for us as teenagers were the weekly 'pick of the pops' and, of course, the evening under the bedclothes listening to the erratic and feeble signal from Radio Luxembourg. Then came Radio City (broadcast from a WW2 fort in the Thames Estuary) and Radio Caroline (moored off the Essex coast), both of which were in international waters. Legislation by Harold Wilson's Government eventually closed them down, resulting in the BBC launching of Radios 1–4 as hurried replacements.

Happy days… now to the book.

AND SO, ON A FINE FRIDAY FEBRUARY afternoon in 1968, I set off from London Victoria on the 14:30 'Boat Train' through the 'Garden of England' to Folkestone. With Bill and Mike, my two far more experienced travellers, spinning tales of previous exploits and contemplating what steam journeys awaited us, I felt a growing well of excitement in anticipation of what lay ahead of us over the next ten days. My only previous expedition abroad was in 1965 – on a package tour with my brother and our parents to the Italian Riviera. During the long overnight coach journey from Oostende to Diano Marina, I can recall looking out of the coach window, approaching our breakfast stop at Basle at six in the morning, and seeing three steam locomotives (West German?) at what was presumably the motive power depot. Nothing further came of that observation; no 'desire' to chase European steam because, during the intervening years, there had been more than enough steam travel to contend with in Britain – until now. I was awoken from my daydreaming by Bill prodding me, saying "Look lively – if we get to the ship's restaurant quickly then the more choice and less waiting". We were at Folkestone Harbour and, having reversed en route, the leading unit (MLV – Motor Luggage Van), in which passengers' luggage was transported, was now on the front. This was detached and should have, under battery power, tripped along the quayside alongside the ship for easy transfer of all the passengers' belongings it contained. It, however, failed and it was left to several porters (as rail operatives were known in those days) to manhandle the contents to the ship. A side benefit of this was the ability to eat our meal without having to chase it around the table – resulting from the ship's movement whilst crossing the channel – as most of it was eaten by the time the *Saint Patrick* had set sail! This unexpected extra 30 minutes gave me a chance to check through my personal belongings in an attempt to ensure that my 'adventure' was adequately catered for: toothbrush, flannel, phrase books, food etc. As regards the latter, and having obviously taken advice from my two more knowledgeable colleagues, sliced bread, butter, jam, fruit and chocolate bars were packed because of the uncertainty and unreliability of food provision wherever we were going. The proposed schedule did not cater for eating or sleeping – just destinations of known steam passenger services – with the proviso of 'where they went, we followed'. Being a BR employee, an International Authority card (to enable reduced fares to be purchased when venturing off-route from our International Free Pass) was necessary – not forgetting the obligatory camera. Mine was misleadingly called a Kodacolor 35 (I could only afford black and white films!) but Bill, being a higher paid clerical officer, had far superior equipment. At the time, resulting from the mishap with my camera in Austria and to fill the missing gaps in my collection, he gave me copies of his shots and alas, some 40 years later, they are the only ones of his currently available.

Finally and perhaps most importantly, was an adequate cash supply. Cash machines had not been thought of at the time and you always lost out to the bureau de change operators (commission-wise) when changing travellers cheques. Actual 10/-, £1 and £5 notes were the answer and, to thwart the currency restrictions on money taken out of the country (the pound was subsequently devalued), a hiding place had to be devised away from the inquisitive eyes of customs/passport officials. Where else but the instep/sole of your foot – inside your socks! Often used over the years as a 'safe place' to keep money away from more accessible places when visiting areas frequented by lowlife personages (pick-pockets/vagrants etc), I can recommend it!

Most of my European visits were started or completed at either Calais or Boulogne. With both Maritime stations having long since ceased to exist, courtesy of the Chunnel, only nostalgic memories of the slow crawl through the docks complex remain. These trains would always be preceded by a port official, on foot, and gesticulating wildly with his flag whilst blowing his whistle furiously at anybody who dared cross in front of them or who had parked their vehicle too close to the track for comfort. Today's health and safety custodians would have nightmares! By the time we arrived at Calais, it was a moonlit evening which, together with the station lighting, only seemed to emphasise what, to me, was the magnificent monster at the front of our train. I was informed that she was one of the three remaining 231G Pacifics – No 97. Looking up in awe (from the lower-than-I-had-been-used-to platform), the scene, to others, must have resembled the well-known Southern Railway poster depicting a schoolboy talking to the driver of a *Holiday Express* about to depart from Waterloo to magical distant destinations. Externally clean, with an array of paraphernalia on the outside, she was a world away from the 'Spam Cans' I had spent many years riding behind. For those readers unaware of what exactly 'Spam Cans' were, it was the nickname given to the Southern Railway, air smoothed, encased, unmodified, Bulleid Light Pacific locomotives that worked throughout the Southern Region of BR for over two decades. There was an air of importance about the dark olive-green and yellow-lined Pacific. The 'motorcycle-goggled' footplate staff were, I subsequently read, held in high esteem by all concerned and looked down with disdain on us 'earthlings' scampering to board the train. The Calais allocations of Pacifics were the pride of the depot, being kept in immaculate condition both externally and, I believe, internally as well. Having been sent to Calais from depots throughout the SNCF system as electrification and dieselisation gradually reduced their duties elsewhere, these Pacifics ended their days working the fast services to/from the ancient capital of Picardy, 104 miles distant – Amiens. Eight Pacifics were required for these trains, with all other semi fast/stopping/relief duties being in the hands of the very capable, but less imposing, 141Rs.

The destination for this, my first of an eventual nine visits to France, was Grenoble. Having crossed from the Nord station at Paris on the Metro, an eclectic mix of antiquated stock and modern stations, we arrived in time for the 23:46 departure from the Lyon station. The combination of its being a Friday night, skiing season and the final day of the Winter Olympics made for an excessively crowded journey. Six to a compartment with legs intertwined, attempted conversation, occasional smiles with the pervading aroma of French cigarettes meant only sporadic sleep was achieved during the seven hour journey. The following is an extract from my tattered notebook:

Upon arrival at Grenoble we enquired from a pretty information girl the whereabouts of the Station Master's office (Bill having previously written to and received a reply from the office as regards steam workings in the area). She duly took us there and, after 30 minutes talking, phoning etc. (all through another girl interpreter), we were taken to the shed where the Shed Master (or whatever title the post held!) took us around himself. On shed were 141Rs 624, 559 and 1104 – of which 624 was photographed, footplated and explained about at length. She was the only one in steam and was to work a freight service later that day. ALL SPECIALS WERE IN THE HANDS OF BORROWED DIESELS! Having gone well out of our way in the hope of steam-powered services, we left the area thoroughly disappointed, heading for the nearest known 'pocket' of steam, Belfort, some 200 miles distant.

After five hours travelling, via Lyon and Dijon, with diesel and electric traction, we arrived at Dole at 16:00. I say 'we' but, somewhere along the line, Mike went off elsewhere – no further reference to him in my 'little red book' was documented. As in Britain, each enthusiast has his or her own targets or requirements. Some specialise in photography; some in haulage; and some are track bashers. With the common – in those days – denominator of steam, it was only at those locations i.e. the Iron Horses' habitat, where groups or individuals met and exchanged notes/sightings, and that acquaintances were renewed – before setting off in different directions pursuing their own personal quests. So there was nothing unusual in Mike's disappearance – just par for the course.

Anyway, back to my travels and my first 141R (of an eventual 43) was caught. 141R17 was working from Dole that day and, having negotiated her way through the freight sidings (engineering work diversion, possibly in connection with impending electrification), thrashed her way eastwards in the gathering gloom for the 28-mile journey with the Besancon portion of the 12:25 from Paris Lyon. Two further 141R-operated steam services were enjoyed before we left the area, changing at Dijon onto the 21:43 (Winter Ski extra) Paris Lyon to Mouries Salins service, which conveyed a portion detached at the junction station of Bellegarde, for Evian-Les-Bains. It was this portion we were interested in, there being a 50/50 chance of steam on the branch to the Lake Geneva resort, famous for its mineral water. No other enthusiast had tried it out – we were the guinea pigs! At 05:30 on a cold Sunday morning, with several diesels standing about, the welcome sight of an oil-fired Annemasse – allocated 141R backing down for the 48-mile trip along the branch – cheered us up no end. A thoroughly enjoyable 1 ½ hours, early morning journey through the foothills of the Chablais Alps was well appreciated – more so, perhaps, after the disappointment of the previous day. This, however, left us looking at Switzerland (necessary to access if we were to continue with our planned itinerary!) from the wrong side of Lake Geneva. I am unable to remember how we discovered it but at 10:00 we caught a privately-owned boat (passports checked en route!) across to Lausanne where, after a trip on a rack metro railway up to the town, we continued on our journey to Italy from the main line station.

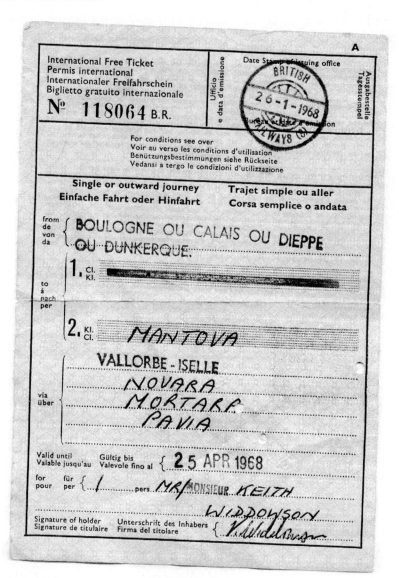

CHAPTER TWO
ITALIAN AFFAIRS
02

THE ALPINE SCENERY, NEVER APPRECIATED FULLY BY the air traveller, on the 91-mile journey through Switzerland from Lausanne to Brig that Sunday morning was, to my mind, exactly as depicted on the front of chocolate box collections – the ones given out as Christmas presents. Snow-capped mountains with fir tree lined sides – all bathed in brilliant sunshine in a cloudless blue sky. As a complete contrast after Brig, where a change of electric traction was made, we plunged into the darkness of the Simplon tunnel. This is the world's seventh longest railway tunnel and, at over 12 miles, is twin bore. Originally opened in 1906, the second bore being added in 1922, events 100 years later to commemorate the occasion included a half hourly shuttle through the tunnel and post bus service over the top (both free!). The southern exit at Domodossola is situated at the confluence of the Bogna and Tocc rivers and is home to over 18,000 people. The station is in effect a minor passenger hub for the area and all International trains (including the prestigious *Venice-Simplon Orient Express*) call there to offload the many tourists for the nearby Italian Alps. As was often the case in my travels, no foot was set outside the station by us during our time there. We weren't there as tourists to see the sights and visit towns etc: we were there for STEAM travel. With over three hours to wait, a glass of wine (when in Rome, do as the Romans do!) was partaken of at the buffet whilst observing the push me/pull you fly – shunting exchange of Swiss/Italian electrics – necessary because of the voltage differences.

We were at Domodossola on the off-chance that the 32-mile secondary route via Omegna had some steam working along it. As always, we selected services shown in the public timetable without a railcar emblem at the top of the column, keeping our fingers crossed in anticipation. Most of the diminishing Italian steam allocations were to be found in the northern lowlands between Torino and Venezia and, with Domodossola being out on a limb, there was a risk, a lot of which were taken throughout my European travels, of diesel haulage. The timetable showed three (out of nine) such services and, with no previous steam sightings during all the time we had spent there, it was with a sense of relief – even justification – that a 66-year-old 640.123 arrived with the 14:23 from Novara. Not that that meant the return working (our 17:22 departure) would also be steam – but the likelihood had improved. Sister locomotive no. 145 duly backed onto the stock (an impressive, by Italian standards, 16 minute turnaround) for our 25-station, three-hour, 55 ¾-mile back-breaking journey on upright, highly polished, wooden seats. It seemed half the Italian Army were aboard this well-patronised two-van/two-coach train, which was assisted from Omegna by another 640 – being attached on the rear. This method of getting locomotives to/from their next duty was often observed – presumably because most routes utilised for such a practice were single tracked, and it was less problematic than running them separately. Unlike the conditions British steam locomotives were being kept in by that year, the Italian veterans (all of which had seen service during both World Wars) were all kept in good (externally, at least) condition. Arriving at the reasonable hour of 8 p.m. enabled us to find a bed for the night quite easily at 1200 lira (£4.70) and, having secured that, as no further steam action was anticipated, we had something to eat. Resulting from the combination of cost and the need to cover as many (often very early morning) steam services as possible, the comfort enjoyed that night was to be the last for five!

Novara is an important commercial centre in the Padan Plain (often referred to as the Po Valley) and many firms have relocated there away from the congestion of nearby Milano. With that fact, together with a population exceeding 100,000, it was inevitable that the requirement for a second station (operated by Le Nord railway – non-state-owned) was deemed necessary – subsequently opening in 2005. The 33-mile 'suburban' branch heading north into the 'Sacred Mountain' town of Varallo Sesia had only two services each way shown as non-railcar. The Italian steam locomotive seemed to delight in working the most inaccessible, inconvenient services possible along branches and an 08:56 departure was a rare welcome exception to this scenario – on this dull dreary Monday morning. 880.167, a 2-6-0T of 1916 vintage, was the motive power – a class not unlike the British USA tank but seemingly more powerful – this particular example emitting an unusual sounding squeak with every exhaust beat! Even then, without being stranded steamless for several hours, we had to alight at Sizzano, a mere 13 ¾ miles along the branch, returning to Novara on one of the characterless 'bog carts'.

Two short railcar journeys via Mortara took us cross-country to the agricultural town of Pavia. Situated on the electrified main line from Milano to Italian Riviera, the likelihood of steam seemed remote. This was all unknown territory for steam enthusiasts with no reports having filtered through the grapevine as to the possibility of any Iron Horse sightings. But wait – a familiar smell of burning coal was drifting across from a small building near the tracks, masquerading as an engine shed. With two hours to kill prior to a possible steam working, we attempted to 'bash' the shed – being told abruptly to apply for a permit from HQ at Milano! There was only one Class 880 in residence anyway. Hopes rose at 12:40 when the 10:23 from Cremona with 880.010 arrived. This stock formed the third train of the day back along this line: our train – the 13:32 for Mantova, and the first shown non-railcar. The 880 previously seen in the distance 'on shed' duly turned up and took us on what can best be described as a leisurely ride across the plains of Italy on a three-hour, 59 ¾-mile journey. At Chignolo Po, an aptly named hamlet where the line crosses a tributary of the river Po itself and a mere 18 miles and one hour from Pavia, we crossed a railcar on an opposite way working. This 'delay' gave us ample time to wander around and take photographs at will. It was only when researching for this book that I read a report in *The Railway World* (1971) stating that 'It is against the law to take photographs on Italian railway property without written permission' – we luckily never came across any officialdom attempting to enforce it. Cremona, perhaps the largest pocket of Italian steam remaining by 1968, was the next important town on this cross-country service. Always attempting to maximise as many runs behind as possible, with different steam locomotives, we did not alight there, going through to Torre Picenardi – a station just short of the next crossing point on the single line to Mantova. The terrain this cross-country train took was flat and apparently subject to severe flooding, justifying the area being known locally as 'The Fens'. A sister 'USA' took us back the 14¼ miles to Cremona where my only sighting of a representative of the diminutive 835 (0-6-0T) class was noted. Most depots throughout Italy still retained at least one working steam locomotive – usually for shunting or standby purposes but Cremona shed surpassed that scenario with representatives from almost every class remaining. The depot was some distance from the station and taking into consideration the weather (for this time of year unusually sunny and warm), as it would have meant carrying our bags and coats, we vetoed the idea. The station was like stepping back in time, with wooden seated compartment coaches and semaphore signals in abundance – not forgetting the multitude of steam locomotives ever present. A return trip northwards to the junction station (of the Treviglio and Brescia routes) of Olmeneta was a more attractive prospect than sightseeing in this historic town and resulted in our ensnaring two more of the lightweight 625 locomotives. Indeed, the only route (out of six) from Cremona which did not have steam services was the Fidenza line. To our delight, our 20:38 departure to Mantova arrived with a Class 685 locomotive, an example of the largest-sized steam class remaining (2-6-2), having previously seen being attached to the rear of a train heading in the opposite direction some three hours earlier. Our posteriors then appreciated 39 miles and 1 ¼ hours of luxury travel in comfortable leather upholstered seats – the first train in over 24 hours that did NOT have either hard or wooden ones! After partaking of some wine and watching Italian TV in the buffet, reality returned and it was back to wooden seats on a Verona-bound steam service at 22:27. This was one of only two non-railcar services per day (the other being the 06:41) over the 23-mile line back to the international electrified main across Northern Italy – last seen 13 hours previously at Novara. We had spent all those hours on secondary routes across 'The Fens' catching runs with seven different steam locomotives – many months had passed since such a quota had been successfully achieved in Britain.

The next service we planned to catch that Tuesday morning was the 04:28 Rovigo to Verona. We were at the wrong end of that 61-mile line and (I hope the reader is following this on the map) to get to Rovigo we had to travel via Bologna. Having fallen asleep on the warm Austria to Roma International train, it was only Bill's alarm clock (being a more experienced traveller than me, he was far better equipped!) that enabled us to scramble off at Bologna at 01:54 in the morning for a 1½ hour fester to await the train over the second part of a triangular night-time journey to Rovigo. It was a mere three minute, cross platform, connection into the local train at Rovigo and having alighted there not realising, in our semi-comatose state, that our train from Bologna had lost time en route, the 'connection' had gone – effectively stranding us. Quick reference to the well-thumbed timetable revealed a stopping electric-hauled service, some 20 minutes later, to Padova on which, during the hour's journey, alternative plans for the day were made. All very Heath

Robinson – constant revision/ alteration totally dependent on events completely out of our control! Searches for non-railcar journeys on branch lines in the area revealed that a 20-mile branch from Vicenza had a 06:28 outward from Schio and a 19:28 return and therefore qualified for attention – possibly steam? An eastbound train to Vicenza (a mere 30 miles from where we were six hours previously!) was caught where we changed for a railcar service to the first station along the branch – Cavazzale. We were rewarded with 625.156 hauling an absolutely wedged commuter train – which somewhat made up for earlier disappointments that morning. Down to 200 lira (80p) between us, we had to wait for the bureau de change to open at nine o'clock before progressing to our final destination in Italy

– Venezia. This time we did have a look around. Ample descriptions of this man-made city abound in all the brochures and books and I can only add that I was in awe of the place. A third of Venetians live on the historic water-encircled city itself – the remainder at the mainland commune of Venice (its internationally recognised name) at Mestre. After some nourishment, we went for the 12:31 departure from Venezia's Saint Lucia Station for Bassano Del Grappa only to find a diesel locomotive at its head. Very disappointed, and with no sign of steam anywhere, we had no alternative but to travel on it. At Castelfranco Veneto, some 25 miles along the route, five separate single routes junctioned with us and whilst we stood there for ten minutes, three other services interconnected with us – an excellent example of coordinated transport planning but NONE was steam! Having arrived at Bassano, and after photographing one of the strange looking Crosti-boilered, side-chimneyed Class 743s (2-8-0) on a freight, hopes rose when 625.134 arrived with a service from Padova. She was duly turned and worked back to Padova with the 16:04 departure – somewhat extending the seven-minute booked stop en route at Cittadella by reversing into some sidings and collecting four vanfits! I am beginning to appreciate now why every line had at least one loco-operated service per day – it was seemingly to cater for such traffic that to us here in Britain would be described as 'wagonload' – eliminated by Dr Beeching as uneconomical. So we headed once again for Venezia, this time for the *Italien-Osterreich Express*, and the next leg of our ten-day European-wide bash. There was, however, one more surprise in store. Having been bitterly disappointed earlier in the day with the dieselisation of a previously thought-to-be steam Bassano service, the least we expected was steam on the other loco-hauled service of the day, the 18:08 departure out of Venezia. Ever the optimists, we had alighted at the Mestre station on the off-chance that it was and, unbelievably, it arrived with double-headed 625s – no way were we letting these go. A quick check with the timetable showed that we could catch this to the first crossing point on the single line, Maerne di Martellago, returning on the very train we were crossing with – which, more worryingly, was the last southbound train of the day. Missing this – and subsequently the International train we had planned to catch – would throw out our itinerary for days. Where there's a will there's a way, and a two-minute connection was made only because, having struggled/forced our way through this crowded commuter service to the rearmost vehicle, with lots of sorry/excuse me expletives resulting from treading on toes and hitting people with our belongings, upon arrival at Maerne we ran around the back of the train and UP THE TRACK to the waiting railcar. Taking into consideration that we had coats, cameras, a case full of food and timetables, it took us all the way into Venezia before we got our breath back!

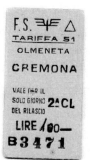
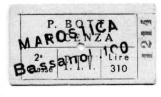

2.01   What can only be described as a leisurely ride across the plains of Northern Italy was undertaken on our first full day in the country on Monday 19th February. Here we are at Chignolo Po, an aptly named hamlet where the line crosses a tributary of the River Po, a mere 18 miles, 1 hour into our journey on the 1332 Pavia to Mantova. Whilst waiting for an opposite way working to cross us on the single line, the driver takes the opportunity to inspect his 52 year old 2-6-OT 880.054.

13

2.02   We had arrived here, at Bassano Del Grappa, somewhat dejectedly behind a diesel from Venice an hour previously and upon seeing 2-6-0 625.156 arriving with the 1309 from Padova on Tuesday 20th February our hopes were raised for her to return – with us aboard. Bill, looking somewhat pensive, had his doubts!

2.03   An example of the largest class of steam locomotive remaining in Italy by 1968 is 2-6-2 685.222 seen here being attached to the rear of the 1545 Mantova to Cadogna at Cremona on Monday 19th February. This method of running an engine from A to B over the many single tracked routes in Italy was often noticed. Some five hours later she worked a service 'in her own right' through Cremona on which we boarded as part of that night's sleeping accommodation.

```
┌─────────────────────────────────────────┐
│         CHAPTER THREE                    │
│          AUSTRIAN          ┌──┐ ┌──┐      │
│         ADVENTURES         │03│           │
└─────────────────────────────────────────┘
```

CHAPTER THREE
AUSTRIAN ADVENTURES
03

USTRIA. FOR THOSE OF YOU WHO HAVE never visited this landlocked country, with its picture postcard scenes of snow-capped peaks and beautiful lakes, you are surely missing out on some of nature's most spectacular scenery. The fir tree coated mountainsides descend to deep valleys where fast-flowing rivers, alongside which road and rail transport links often run parallel, lead to unexpected hubs of civilisation nestling amongst foothills of Alpine magnificence. Although suffering far heavier snowfalls in deep winter than we are ever likely to experience in Britain, the train traveller rarely suffers disruption on a scale endured here when 'the wrong type of snow' falls. Other than winter sports devotees, who else would visit the country in February when, if not suitably attired, the cold permeates every bone in your body when not in an indoors environment? Why, steam train enthusiasts – that's who!

I initially wondered why Bill chose to visit Austria in the February of 1968 as part of a European-wide steam bash. When meeting again to prepare this book, he explained that it was all to do with the previous year's quota of foreign travel passes – use them or lose them – which retained three months' validity. The itinerary undertaken, and spending only two out of nine nights between clean sheets, was a test for the most hardened steam follower – the remaining nights being on trains/platforms or in waiting rooms. For nourishment (in Austria at least) any station of significance always contained a buffet/refreshment room. These establishments were often the meeting point – a social centre, even – for the local population, most of whom were not train travellers. Fortuitously, each buffet seemed to have a cauldron of a piping hot goulash-type meat stew on the go – which, when taking into consideration the bitter temperatures we endured, was most welcome. The schedule did not allow for hours to be wasted in restaurants so the alternative 'food', when the aforementioned 'goulash' was not available, was beer, bread rolls (for which we had exported jam and rapidly deteriorating butter), chocolate bars and the occasional fruit. An added problem, courtesy of the OBB, (Osterreichische Bundesbahnen – Austrian Federal Railways) was their decree, with temperatures below freezing, that all water supplies on the secondary local services be turned off – presumably to avoid any frost damage to the systems. This resulted in numerous successful occasions when Bill and I retained several seats to ourselves, even on the most crowded rush hour services, not perhaps, unsurprisingly, resulting from our 'odour'.

Before progressing into the tour undertaken that winter, perhaps a brief synopsis of the OBB system we encountered would be appropriate. By the time of my first visit approximately 35% (1,350 miles) of the OBB were electrified with the route between Graz and the Yugoslavian border town of Spielfeld Strab under conversion. Authorisation for further electrification had already been granted for lines in the

Hieflau and Wampersdorf areas thus increasing to 45% (85% of the traffic carried) the total number of converted routes. Another aspect noted during our travels was that many stations, particularly in the cities, were of modern designs; indeed seemingly too grand for the traffic dealt with. This was, of course, a legacy of the widespread destruction vented during World War II.

Progressing onto the steam locomotive scene (they were, after all, the reason for the visits), the most numerous class remaining were the Class 52 2-10-0 tender locomotives. These were to be found spread throughout the remaining half a dozen or so 'pockets' of steam in the country. The need for tender locomotives, during the final phase of steam locomotive builds in the 1920s, was negated by widespread electrification and all subsequent designs were of the tank variety. They weren't all, however, the size I was used to seeing in Britain – some of them were huge, presumably built to cope with the tough terrain they encountered throughout their lives in this mountainous country. The representatives I came across during my travels that year were: Class 77 (1912/27) 4-6-2T; Class 78 (1931) 4-6-4T; Class 86 (1928/43) 2-8-2T, not forgetting their smaller sisters, Class 91 (1897/1907) 2-6-0T; Class 93 (1927/1931) 2-8-2T; and the rack Class 97 (1890/1908) 0-6-2T.

Having set the scene; let me now take the reader with me on my Austrian adventure! Travelling from Italy, we entered Austria at the border crossing point of Tarvisio in the early hours of Wednesday 21st February aboard the *Italien-Osterreich Express*. Apparently customs/passports/tickets were all inspected on several occasions en route and, upon confirming with Bill whether I was with him (I was sound asleep!), officials seemed satisfied enough not to wake me. Arriving at Wien Sudbahnhof at 06:50, we eventually located the 07:06 local electric unit to Ganserndorf, in the nick of time, departing from one of the underground platforms at this massive terminus. Even that wasn't straightforward because, at the midway point of that 44-minute journey, at Floridsdorf, the rear portion (which we unwittingly were in) was detached, and we only just made the 'correct' front four cars by throwing a bag in between the closing doors to prevent departure without us!

And so, at Ganserndorf, my first Austrian steam awaited – one of the 1927-built 2-8-2Ts, 93.1422. I was to eventually collect runs behind ten different examples of these compact tank locomotives – all Mistelbach allocated. This wonderful 'model railway' system, with Mistelbach at the centre, comprised numerous routes which seemingly meandered at will through the flat uninspiring plains of the north east corner of the country – referred to geographically as Lower Austria. Each of these lines had three or four trains per day interconnecting with each other whenever they met – some without trains between the early hours of the morning until midday. The obviously poor economics of these services must have eventually been realised because reference to the present OBB system map shows that only ONE route has survived – Wien/Mistelbach/Laa an der Thaya. Indeed the 17-mile section north of Mistelbach was electrified in 2006 and added to the Wien Metro system. As if to highlight the inefficiency back in 1968, a mere nine miles into our journey, at Grob Schweinbarth, we changed locomotives! Studying the relevant timetables whilst researching for this book revealed that each of the four lines radiating from this junction station had between three and six services per day, between the hours of 04:49 and 20:10, when periodically (was it luck or astute planning?) they occasionally interconnected. The 08:00 Ganserndorf to Mistelbach service which we were aboard stopped there from 08:32 to 09:12 (yes, 40 minutes) during which time the station awoke from its slumbers to become a hive of activity. Our locomotive came off, destined to return to Ganserndorf on an 08:56 starting service and, after the two other services had departed, the replacement locomotive, 93.1358, shunted us to the sidings where we attached five wagons and proceeded to 'play' with them. Some were placed in other sidings and some onto the waiting 08:56 Ganserndorf train. After eventually running out of wagons to 'play with', we continued on to the hub of the 150-mile system at Mistelbach – having taken two hours twelve minutes for 13½ miles! You couldn't make it up!

Ignoring the saying 'never drink alcohol before the sun is over the yard-arm' (12 noon), a timetable study session to plan the day's 'moves' was undertaken upon arrival whilst enjoying a ½ litre of lager costing, in today's money, 7½ p! It was often the case that the only time we set foot off railway property, when visiting the various towns or cities on our travels, was to locate an alternative station. Mistelbach, lying about halfway between the Austrian capital and the Iron Curtain border, was no exception – we weren't there to see the sights or whatever was available in this town of 10,000 inhabitants – no; we wanted to find the motive power depot where the majority of remaining representatives of the Class 93 locomotive were allocated. Unchallenged, we visited the shed where three locos were in steam, including 93.1417, the only member of the class we witnessed fitted with an oblong Giesl ejector, before a fill-in trip to Prinzendorf-Rannersdorf (on the Huhenau route)

19

yielded two further catches of the class. An entry in my notebook stating 'we will not try asking for a ticket to this place too often' indicated possible problems in making the booking clerk understand our requests for privilege tickets! It has to be emphasised at this point that some services were worked by railcars (as always, conveniently indicated at the column head in the public timetable) and much careful planning took place over many litres of beer in station buffets to avoid them! A short distance away was the 'main line' station from where our next train took us to the northernmost extremity of the system – the spa town of Laa an der Thaya. During the 28-minute turn around there (same train/same loco/same train crew), the driver took an interest in what two foreigners were doing at this non-tourist outpost (i.e. taking photographs) and through an interpreter friend of his offered us a ride up front. This offer was gratefully accepted but could only be taken one at a time because of the limited space on the footplate. Concern about a four-minute connection at Enzersdorf (a junction station en route back to Mistelbach) evaporated when the train crew, upon arrival there, changed trains themselves and worked the very branch connection to Poysdorf we wanted! Although no other passengers were aboard the branch connection, it became obvious after arrival at Poysdorf (the destination of our free pass from Britain) why it ran. It formed the return 15:10 departure and was totally invaded by school children who, when espying us, swarmed around us like refugees in Africa when food is distributed – asking for souvenirs. The only 'spare' items we had on us were several tubes of sweets which were eagerly accepted. I often wonder whether their parents believed them when they returned home excitedly proclaiming having met two soot-faced (from the footplate), smelly (lack of water on trains) Englishmen handing out sweets! We would probably have been arrested in today's PC world. The sleep-inducing 45-mile trip back to Wien (we had had no respite from the bitterly cold cloudy conditions for nearly nine hours) was behind my first Class 77. This class was subsequently discovered in two other locations visited in Austria and, together with the Class 52 tender locomotives, appeared to be the most widely spread of the remaining examples of steam. A short trip on the Metro to the Praterstern station enabled us to catch two further 77s on north-easterly bound suburban services destined for Bernhardsthal and Mistelbach – the latter being shown to be a railcar in the timetable – before returning to Wien for a welcome hot meal – the first for several days!

Suitably refreshed, our next train, the 22:05 *Balkan Express* from Wien, took us the 142 miles south to the border station with Yugoslavia at Spiefeld Strab – we being rudely awoken en route and 'gripped' 32 Schillings (£2) for being off route, correctly as it happened, from our free passes! Arriving at Spiefeld at 02:19 hours on the Thursday morning, whilst attempting to keep warm during the two-hour wait, we witnessed the Yugoslavian Class 06 locomotives coming in with both passenger and freight services from the south, both of us vowing to return one day! Between 04:25 (doesn't Austrian commuting start early!) and 08:30 hours, we blitzed the local passenger services between Spiefeld Strab and Austria's second largest city, Graz, catching one x 77, one x 78 (4-6-4T) and two x 52s. At Karlsdorf, an intermediate station along the line, we copped 52.7015 – unusual in the fact that she was without the normal smoke deflectors. A visit to Messendorf (on the Gleisdorf line from Graz) in the hope of steam proved fruitless – although one of the trains was unusual in that it was hauled by what can only be described as a fast speed diesel shunting locomotive!

We then made our way to Leoben for what was hoped to be the highlight of the Austrian leg of our tour – the 12:10 departure to Eisenerz over the Tyrol. This steeply graded rack-operated line was built to convey iron ore from the Erzberg mine (located off the 'main line' at the summit station of Prabichl) to the blast furnaces at Vordernberg and Donawitz (Leoben). The 12:10 departure from Leoben Hbf was in the hands of 52.3688 for the ten miles to Vordernberg – which was a bonus because not only was the line electrified but the same service was noted the following day with an electric locomotive. As we began to climb, the snow became noticeably thicker and upon arrival at Vordernberg, the expected change to a rack-equipped Class 97 0-6-2T materialised. Even today, after all those years, I can still recall the 13-mile ride over the Austrian Tyrol as perhaps one of life's most memorable experiences – 1½ hours of sheer exhilaration. The diminutive-looking but obviously up-to-the-task tank engine propelled the two coaches and one van up to the 3,500ft summit at Prabichl before running around and leading the train down to Eisenerz. Another memorable, but subsequently disastrous, 'event' was that the film in my camera became snagged and I had to expose and disentangle it – the result being a reliance on Bill for copies of all photographs taken up to then! The Class 97s, which also worked the town service up to Vordernberg Markt, survived until the mid-Seventies when, with the rerouting of the iron ore traffic via Hieflau, the need for the line disappeared and it was subsequently closed. However, in 1990 it was reopened and operated as a privately run 'museum line' utilising specially adapted adhesion railcars and trailers – and still runs (at the time of writing) two return trips per day for the burgeoning tourist traffic.

The sole remaining examples of Class 86 (2-8-2T) were allocated at Hieflau, a wonderfully picturesque setting surrounded by mountains, and were seemingly confined to duties on the Eisenerz branch line. 86.781 provided a five-minute schoolkid-laden connection out of the aforementioned Leoben train and, similarly to our experience at Poysdorf the previous day, we became the centre of attention again. Everything (with the exception of one return railcar working per day) was steam at Hieflau and a mini bash of services over the next three hours produced runs with three consecutively numbered 78s and one 52. A 'desperate' move, made purely to catch runs with as many locos as possible, was to travel to the first stop out of Hieflau on the Selzthal line – Kummerbrucke Halt. This turned out to be a bus stop, shelter type, unstaffed halt provided, presumably, for the dam keeper on the nearby River Enns. The double headed 16:58 Selzthal to Wien express was shown to call there upon request and I am certain the pilot driver only saw us frantically waving at the last moment. We had deliberately activated the one station light and were waving our arms and bags above our heads – anything to attract his attention. In the gathering gloom of dusk combined with falling snow the long train screeched to a halt with only the last two vehicles being able to be boarded! How we would have dealt with being stranded there begs the question – but reference via today's internet shows the B146 road running nearby and so we could perhaps have hitched a lift back to civilisation. This train took us the short distance back to Hieflau where more 86s were caught on the Eisenerz services. Hopping on and off steam trains, catching a seemingly endless supply of 'new' (i.e. never travelled with before) engines took me back to those splendid days at Southampton or Preston or Bradford where similar scenarios were often enacted.

Back to Austria, and having seen, earlier that day at Leoben, that the 09:40 Selzthal to Bruck train was being hauled by steam, plans were then made to travel to Selzthal from Hieflau (hope you're following all this on the map!) in order to travel on that service the following day. Arriving at Selzthal at 20:00 that evening, a bed for the night was found after enquiring from 'someone' on the platform who, it became obvious, was an owner of a nearby gasthof. He was also, it turned out, an engine driver and over a few beers that evening an interesting conversation in pidgin English/German ensued.

Friday morning dawned bright and clear and a breathtaking view of snow-capped mountains was revealed upon opening the curtains. After a superb night's sleep (only the second between warm/clean sheets in seven days) followed by a decent sized breakfast, further discussion took place with the owner as to whether the 09:40

departure to Bruck an der Mur was steam operated and he was adamant that it was 'elecktra'. He was, luckily for us, proved wrong (shortage of 'elecktras' perhaps) and my longest Austrian steam ride (56½ miles – 2½ hours) was enjoyed with 77.285 under the wires. Resulting from the fact that it was operating to an electric schedule, timekeeping was, at one point, 20 minutes behind – this itself providing a photographic opportunity at a crossing point on the single line where preference was given to a Germany-bound service. Joining the main line at St Michael we then progressed some 25 miles back up towards Wien as far as Murzzuschlag where, it was rumoured, some services on the 6¾-mile Neuberg branch were worked by the 1897-built Class 91 2-6-0T locomotives. Sure enough, we were lucky enough to catch No 40 performing the honours that afternoon and, with time to kill before our overnight train to France, a second return trip along the branch was made. Although sister No 107 together with a Class 392 0-8-0T were in steam at Murzzuschlag, No 40 stayed on the shuttle – still, beggars can't be choosers! This branch was dieselised by 1972 but has subsequently closed completely. The International train to Basle did not call at such a lowly station as Murzzuschlag so we travelled back to Leoben for it. The 360-mile journey, which took us through the principality country of Liechtenstein (middle of the night/no apparent passport check!), took 13 hours and, although being completely worn out, we only slept fitfully, not helped by the many reversals en route, on our way to more French steam and then home to Blighty.

3.01　With time to kill at Mistelbach whilst waiting for one of the somewhat sparse services operated over the North East Austrian 'system' the opportunity was taken to bash the shed on Wednesday 21st February. No one challenged us whilst we walked around and we photographed three examples of the 2-8-2T 60 year old Class 93 locomotives (1386, 1417 and 1349) which monopolised the non railcar services. 93.1417 (centre) was the only example we saw which was fitted with a giesl ejector.

3.02   Can you feel the cold? A perfect example of the services run over this 'model railway system' throughout the flat uninspiring plains of North Eastern Austria. 93.1360 is seen here approaching Prinzendorf Rannersdorf on a cold, freezing Wednesday 21st February with the 1105 Hohenau to Mistelbach. The entire system, excepting the 'main line' from Laa an der Thaya via Mistelback to Wein, has subsequently closed.

3.03   Thursday 22nd February saw us at Leoben and although the 1210 departure to Eisenerz was 'under the wires' for the first 10 miles of its journey to Vordernberg, we were blessed with 52.3688 – a 2-10-0 freight locomotive. This train was seen the following day with an electric locomotive so we were indeed fortunate.

3.04   Here at Prabichl (3,500 ft) the snow lay thick and the 60 year old rack engine (0-6-2T) 97.209 having 'pushed' us up from Vordernberg with the 1210 Leoben to Eisenerz had now run round the train to 'lead us down' the other side of the mountain on Thursday 22nd February. An absolutely memorable experience of crossing the Austrian Tyrol often standing on the open verandah at the end of the coach enjoying the views and listening to the tank locomotive struggling up the incline. This journey can still be made today albeit in specially adapted railcars.

27

3.05   Having arrived after dark at Selzthal and desperate for shelter from the bitterly cold conditions, we chanced across a Gasthof owner on the station. A few beers with him that night before retiring meant that no notice of our surroundings had been taken and this view the following morning, Friday 23rd February, was what greeted us upon our opening the curtains. Surely a Christmas card scene!

3.06   Presumably resulting from a shortage of electric locomotives, the 0940 Selzthal to Bruck a d Mur, seen here at an unrecorded intermediate calling point was on Friday 23rd February worked by 4-6-2T 77.285. At this point she, being unable to maintain the electric schedule, was running some 20 minutes late and Bill took the opportunity to photograph the train (with yours truly hanging out of the window) whilst preference over the single line was given to an opposite way Germany bound express.

CHAPTER FOUR

ONE OF
CHAUMONT'S FINEST

04

S O, HAVING TRAVELLED OVER 3,300 MILES IN the preceding eight days, we re-entered France at Basle, heading once more for the Belfort/Mulhouse 'pocket' of steam which we had visited a week earlier. The difference with this visit was that by being that much earlier in the day, we hoped we would catch a run with one of the Chaumont-allocated 'Mountains' – classified in France as a 241P. The 4-8-2 wheel arrangement is recognised throughout the world as a 'Mountain' type and, with an ever-increasing diesel presence throughout France, was becoming increasingly hard to track down. The 11:36 Basle to Paris Est, an expected duty for one, was taken over at Mulhouse by a diesel (!!!) locomotive! Had all the Ps gone? Reference to the timetable showed us we had the ability to get as far east towards Paris as Langres before passing another possibility for a 241P – the 12:25 opposite way working from the capital. Having effectively put all our eggs in one basket, with no alternative steam arrangements available, we were more than pleased to see 241P32 duly arrive with the Paris train. If I thought the Pacific at Calais, over a week previously, was huge – this machine was monstrous. The 140-mile Chaumont to Mulhouse section of the main line from Paris to Basle was not considered, at the time, sufficiently viable for electrification resulting in six of these 241P Mountains having an extended stay of execution – again, as always, whilst awaiting an adequate supply of diesels. With the snow by now falling silently and persistently, this massive 241P effortlessly, and surprisingly quietly, quickly achieved and maintained the 75mph maximum permitted for the class – 241P31 being passed whilst working the 14:10 ex-Basle. The somewhat lacklustre vista of the plains of Eastern France, coupled with the onset of dusk, inevitably led to some much-needed sleep – always satisfactorily deeper when behind steam power!

The rear portion of this Paris to Basle train was detached at Mulhouse to form a departure over the border to Berne – capital city of Switzerland. This public transport link between the two countries – a mere two trains each way and obviously not promoted – was eventually closed in 1996. Delle, the actual border crossing point, was, however, reconnected in 2006 with the Swiss transport system, and recent plans (2009) envisage the French side to be reopened and electrified in connection with a new high speed line in the Belfort area. 141R244 worked our one-coach service train the 14¼ miles to Delle – conveniently connecting into the second train of the day in the opposite direction – the 17:15 from Berne. Both of these one-coach trains were exchanged from a Swiss electric locomotive to French steam but, surprisingly, a different 141R took us back to Belfort. The 20:30 Belfort to Besancon train was then caught, it being exactly one week since we were last on it, changing then onto the homeward bound Paris train; and with the train being over thirty minutes late from Dijon (due into Paris at 04:27), I was unsure exactly when we arrived because, upon awakening, no one else was around! Also not noted was how we crossed to the Nord station. Surely the Metro wasn't running then – we must have walked!

The first train on that Sunday morning towards the Channel ports was the 06:57 departure and, not wishing to waste any opportunity for steam runs, a return trip was made to the Clapham Junction equivalent of the Paris Nord suburban system – St Denis. These services were powered by 141TC class locomotives which always stayed on the country end of the push/pull-fitted fixed set formation trains. The 06:57 departure, being a 'semi', was taken over by a 141R at Amiens which then ploughed through the recently white-mantled fields of Northern France created by the overnight blizzard of snow – eventually terminating at Boulogne Ville where we changed onto the following 08:10 'fast' from Paris. This was in the hands of one of the other type of Pacifics allocated at Calais that I had yet to see – 231K82. Although Bill had decided to go straight home from Calais, having met a couple of friends there, I succumbed to the desire for one further steam run – by catching a railcar to Hazebrouck for the inwards *Italia Express*. During the hour wait there, a French 'chippy' was located, and the large portions of 'pommes frites' were ravenously devoured. I returned to the station where the train, having departed from Milano at 21:50 the previous night had, by the time it had reached Hazebrouck at 14:00 the following day, collected an assortment of multicoloured coaches from

various countries. Although Austrian, French and Hungarian vehicles were included in the formation, we always headed for the 'plush' Italian ones with their leather-upholstered seats, drop-down arms and spacious compartments offering greater leg room. The final 40 miles of its journey were in the hands of one of Boulogne's large allocation of American Mikados which were to be regularly used by myself to 'finish off' the many either long or short European bashes over the next two years. Although a somewhat rough crossing on the *Invicta* was endured, it didn't dampen my reflections on what had been achieved over the previous ten days. A wonderful adventure – travelling over 4,000 miles with 52 different steam locomotives for the princely sum of £21.

CHAPTER FIVE

THE BASTILLE 'STORMING'

05

T HE MAIN PURPOSE OF THIS TRIP, COMMENCING on Friday 15th March, was to blitz the Paris Bastille suburban services – the last outpost of the once numerous 1913-built 2-8-2 Mikado 141TB class of suburban tanks. Most of the Est area suburban services were electrified by 1962 but there remained an isolated 13-mile branch from Paris Bastille to Boissy St Leger. Its days as a steam operated service were numbered because the route, which was basically an hourly service, was to be incorporated within the Paris suburban system as RATP (Regie Autonome des Transports Parisiens – the city's metro system) Red Route A2 – the actual implementation taking place 21 months hence.

We (Dave and I) left London Victoria on the prestigious *Golden Arrow*, albeit in the standard accommodation, and after yet another rough crossing of the Channel (yes, it was *Invicta* again) we continued through to Paris on the *La Fleche D'Or* – enjoying a thoroughly lively run with 231G81 en route, arriving there in the peak at 17:25. We could have bashed the Bastille services then and there but this would have left us without overnight accommodation – other than station benches at Paris terminus! Having by then settled into a career on BR involving train planning, my 'specialist skills' were brought into use. My appetite for more runs with the Mountains having been whetted after the previous month's visit to the Belfort area saw us heading out of Paris Lyon on the 18:57 to Clermont Ferrand – to home in on the pocket of 241Ps allocated to the Massif Central part of France. This train, at the junction station of Moret les Sablons, some 42 miles from Paris on the main line to Dijon, was booked to be worked forward by one of ten 241Ps based at the very centre of this 'Bourbonnais line' – Nevers. We were not disappointed and pleasantly surprised when, as an unexpected bonus, all services exchanged locomotives at Nevers. I am unable to tell from my notes whether what happened then was an instant decision or planned but, upon arriving at Riom at 23:57, eight miles short of Clermont Ferrand – the train's destination - a three-minute cross-platform connection was enacted into an opposite way service back to Paris, also 241P-hauled. Unlike our last train which was routed via Vichy, a town of certain notoriety during World War Two when the Nazi regime made it their French HQ during their four years of occupancy, the returning train, the 16:20 from Beziers, was routed via Gannet and Montlucon reaching electrification at Vierzon – the junction station with the Toulouse main line. Although, throughout my travels in this area, all 241Ps seen were during the night hours, it was obvious, like Calais, that they were the pride of Nevers shed – being kept, as compared with the 141Rs allocated at the same depot, in immaculate condition. Arriving back into Paris at six a.m., we considered that our overnight accommodation trip had been successfully accomplished – with over 350 miles of steam haulage to boot!

It was now Saturday morning and after a brisk walk we arrived at the Paris Bastille station – a suburban terminus somewhat unusually perched above street level. Reminding me of London's Broad Street, which also had an air of neglect about it, we encountered our first 141TB simmering away at the head of the 06:25 departure to Boissey St Leger. These locomotives were worked bunker-first (country end) in push/ pull mode and, with a diagrammer's mentality to the fore, we managed to obtain runs with all five in circulation that morning. With single-line working, speed restrictions and track-slewing diversions taking place throughout the runs in connection with the aforementioned electrification, these feisty tanks 'stormed' away from each station/ speed slack on these services to and from the Bastille – scene of the 18th century riot that was the catalyst for the French Revolution. The viaduct immediately outside the terminus is all that remains – converted into a pedestrian walkway.

Having achieved our objective of that trip we now crossed Paris again – to my fourth different capital terminus, Paris Est. This move was a gamble. Had the 12:25 departure, successfully caught with a 241P further into its journey last month, succumbed to diesel haulage from Chaumont? Only 164 miles later, when 241P26 was backing on, did we breathe a sigh of relief. This summed up a lot of my travels during 1968 in France. It was the last year of main line steam in many parts of the country and vast distances needed to be covered in the hope that steam still was active at each destination visited. After arriving at Belfort, we spoke to a French enthusiast who informed us that the 14:10 from Basle (seen on the previous visit with a 'Mountain') had gone diesel. Indeed, a mere eight weeks later the 241Ps had no regular passenger work rostered and only 241P32 escaped withdrawal by being transferred to Le Mans. He also informed us that there had been occasional reports that the Delle portion off the Paris train had been worked by a 141P (we weren't, however, that lucky), an ubiquitous, but welcome, 141R being that evening's power. All this, however, was due to change in the near future – with electrification plans for the Dole/Besancon/Belfort route replacing 52 steam locomotives with a mere 20 electrics already authorised.

Arriving back into Paris that Sunday morning, for some reason we did not, as previously, undertake the St Denis visit prior to catching the 06:57 Boulogne train. The Montreal-built 141R1285 taking over at Amiens was in great form, not only waking up any line-side residents attempting a lie-in but also clouding the French countryside with what I thought was thick oily smog. I have subsequently read that she was one of a batch of original oilfired locos converted by SNCF to coal in 1957 – you could have fooled me – but then I didn't hang out of the window on this cold morning to ascertain either way! These solid dependable machines, built in America/Canada after World War II to get France moving again, became the final steam locomotives in SNCF (**Société Nationale des Chemins de fer Français** – French National Railways) service some years later, 12 of which have survived, in one form or another, into preservation. The 08:10 'fast' behind us had the usual immaculate Pacific (231K31) on it and, indeed, a relief running in front had another, 231K44. As was becoming the norm, the standard 'let's have one more steam run before home' trip back to Hazebrouck was made – before yet another rough crossing with *Invicta*.

5.01   I only caught two of this particular Pacific class. Here 4-6-2 231G81 is about to be
        detached from the southbound 'Golden Arrow' at Amiens on Friday 15th March. She
        (together with the K variations) were to last just 10 more months before dieselisation of
        the fast services between here and the English ports was implemented.

5.02   The 13 mile isolated suburban route from Paris Bastille to Boissey St Leger was the last
home of the Class 141TB 2-8-2T 1913 built class. With electrification work in hand for
the line to be incorporated with the RATP Metro system, a visit just had to be made. Here,
on Saturday 16th March, the 0900 (457) and 1000 (477) services await departure from
the Bastille station on this sunny spring morning.

5.03　　I was completely bowled over at the size of this 241P 4-8-2 'Mountain' as emphasised by the adjacent driver. I had never come across such a powerful, surprisingly silent, looking monster – one of which I believe survives in preservation. On Saturday 16th March one of Chaumont's six, No 26, backs onto the 1225 Paris Est to Basle/Berne at her home station. She was to effortlessly work the heavy train the 111 miles to Mulhouse – but within a few months was dispatched to the breaker's yard.

THE FIRST GERMAN INVASION

06

"**D**ON'T PANIC, CAPTAIN MAINWARING – WE MIGHT just get there in time" could have been the scenario when, having been alerted to the imminent demise of a large pocket of DB 03 (Deutsche Bundesbahn – West German National Railways) Pacifics, we (Bill and I) set off from London Victoria on Friday 17th May. The target was an assault on the 38 ½ mile route between Aachen and Monchengladbach, both locations being in the Federal State of North Rhine – Westphalia. Aachen, the westernmost city in Germany was, during World War II, systematically destroyed by the Nazis to keep it out of Allied hands – and subsequently became the first German city to be liberated in October of 1944. Once an industrial city of major importance, the IT industry now is its main employer. At the other end of our targeted line was Monchengladbach – originally named after the Gladbach 'river' which nowadays runs subterraneously under the city. To distinguish it from another similarly named town it was renamed Munchen-Gladbach in 1888, Monchen-Gladbach in 1950 then being given its present name in 1960. The railway between the two cities had, by our visit, all the required paraphernalia associated with overhead electrification in situ and was to be energised a mere two weeks hence. Having crossed to Oostende on the *Reine Astrid*, an uneventful 174-mile journey aboard the *Tauern Express* found us arriving at Aachen at 00:57 on the Saturday morning. Over my train-travelling life, both for pleasure and commuting, I must have spent thousands of hours 'waiting' at stations – and here were 3½ hours more! There were quite a few V100 diesels around and, ominously, one powered our first train – the 04:30 to Monchengladbach. There wasn't a need for concern, however, as my first West German steam engine, in the form of 03.087, was on the 06:13 service returning back down the line to Aachen. With reversals required at both ends of this route on most through- trains, one wondered why this 'gap' in the electrified network had not been 'plugged' before. The next few hours were spent carefully covering every possible steam working by hopping on and off at intermediate stations en route including Monchengladbach's second station at Rheydt, the junction station for Koln, resulting in five catches of these handsome 03 Pacifics. Noted on freights were representatives of Classes 41, 50 and 52 – with stored Class 55s seen in sidings at a location not noted at the time. Unbeknown to us, before our arrival on the scene, was the fact that certain Monchengladbach to Koln local trains were also steam operated and so, amending any plans originally made, at 11:15 we set off to Germany's fourth largest city – Koln. Once described as 'the world's greatest heap of debris' by a German architect after intensive Allied bombing, Koln is now the vibrant centre of the Rheinland. Although famed for its cathedral, Eau de Cologne perfume and week-long annual carnival, none of those 'attractions' was sufficient reason to leave railway station premises – we were there for steam! Not alighting at the main Hauptbahnhof station, we crossed over the River Rhine to Koln's other station – Deutz. This station is basically used as a relief to the bottleneck scene at the main station, with some through services calling at the Deutz instead.

Capitalising on our unexpectedly new venue of Koln, a trip down the Moselle Valley route to Euskirchen was made prior to returning northwards, thus collecting runs with a second class of West German steam I hadn't seen before – the 01s. The 14-coach train was dealt with dismissively by this equally handsome stronger brother to the 03s. At Euskirchen, the rear four coaches were detached; and attached to the rear of our returning train some 50 minutes later – a clever strengthening move, presumably to cater for heavy usage over the busiest section of the line. A surprising turn-up for the book, later that day, was a Class 50 on what was indicated in the timetable as a railcar-operated service to Kaldenkirchen. This border crossing point to Venlo, Holland, being a mere 2½ miles away, has subsequently lost its importance, now that all member countries of the EEC allow free movement between themselves, but is still, however, being heavily used by freight traffic. The steam working did not return to Monchengladbach and so we had to suffer a V100 diesel journey before two further steam runs, albeit with locomotives caught earlier that day, brought us back to our starting point of some 24 hours previous – Aachen.

Another long wait, this time 2½ hours, was endured on that Sunday morning before boarding the 03:02 *Nord Express* for Paris. Just three hours later, having arrived at the border station (Belgium/France) of Erquelinnes, the train was not able to progress any further due to one of France's regular activities so often initiated without any prior notice – a general strike! It was not just rail; it was everything so there was not even any power in the overhead wires! Bill did well here, using the logic "let's get away before total chaos ensues", by referring quickly to the timetable which revealed that a local train to Charleroi would leave within half an hour, where a connection to Brussels was available. By changing there into an Oostende service, and subsequently the *Kongihn Fabiola* car ferry into Dover Eastern Docks, we caught the very train we would have connected into at Dover Marine as we would have if we had come, as originally planned, from Paris – albeit having lost out on SNCF Pacific haulage from Amiens.

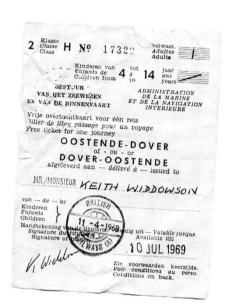

6.01   Monchengladbach sees the departure of a 'footex' for Koln on Saturday 18th May with 4-6-2 03.251 in charge. Not appreciating some services from here to Koln were steam operated, we veered away from our original plan (staying on the Monchengladbach to Aachen services which were to be electric powered two weeks later) to travel to Koln and caught her working normal service trains later that day.

6.02   Having ventured away from our planned Monchengladbach area bash to Koln we then
        further varied our itinerary to include a couple of runs down the Mosel valley route to
        Euskirchen. Here 4-6-2 01.008 rests whilst an extra four coaches are added to the rear of
        the 1135 Saarbrucken to Emden service on Saturday 18th May.

M Y APPETITE FOR WEST GERMAN STEAM HAVING been whetted by the visit detailed in the previous chapter, it was a mere ten days later, on the 29th May, that Bill and I set off out of London Victoria – this time to South West Germany – for hopefully a great many Dampfloks to be caught! We became of 'no fixed abode' for the six-day epic – all overnights spent on stations or trains. The departure of the *Reine Astrid* was held back an extra 30 minutes to collect passengers for the cancelled Calais boat – the French strike which had disrupted our returning journey earlier that month still going on. It was very hot and sunny inland but out in the Channel the thick fog did not help the ship's timekeeping, causing the connecting 21:10 *Tauern Express* to depart Oostende over 40 minutes late.

It being under a month away from the longest day, the sun was well and truly up by the time we arrived at the city of Mannheim at 05:33 (32 minutes late) on the Thursday morning. The first objective was to visit Weinheim, a town a mere 15 miles north on the main line to Frankfurt, and good fortune was bestowed upon us in that the local train connections held for us. This enabled us to arrive there just in time for one of the few loco-operated trains each day along the 10 ½ mile branch to Furth. There were only 18 Class 65 (2-8-4T) locomotives ever built, and of the three pockets that these locomotives were allocated to, the best possible chance of passenger work was here at Weinheim. Our second piece of good fortune within half an hour came in the form of 65.002, which was working the 06:06 branch departure that morning. This seemingly oversized tank engine stormed along the branch, letting all and sundry know she was coming with her resonant hooter and

44

cowbell being operated frequently. By 1971, all remaining members of that class had been transferred to Aschaffenburg to work on the Miltenberg branch and even that was short-lived because, a mere two years later, the class was but a memory. Most 'services' on this branch line to Furth had either a bus or railcar symbol at the head of the column so we considered ourselves most fortunate with the catch and hoped that it would prove to be just the start we needed for our voyage of exploration into uncharted territories that lay ahead.

We then made our way to the city of Heidelberg which, having somehow escaped being blitzed during the intensive Allied bombing campaign of World War II, has retained the atmosphere of the 17th century rebuild, with its cobbled streets and stone bridges allegedly attracting romantic weekenders in their hordes. Upon arrival, we purchased the equivalent of a rail rover, which necessitated a visit to a photo booth, for the princely sum of DM 46 (£5). Using the ever-present phrase book, we learnt from the small print on the back of the rover that we were allowed to use the first-class accommodation on all but the fastest trains – and, boy, did we make the most of that facility, especially on the overnights and, in particular, using berthed stock in Stuttgart platforms as our sleeping accommodation! On that first day, we confined ourselves to the two routes between Heidelberg and the pivotal, from our steam catches point of view, axis of Heilbronn. Although both routes were scenically attractive, passing as they did through towns and villages surrounded by thickly forested hills, perhaps the more northerly of the two, via Eberbach, enhanced by the often parallel River Neckar, was more so. Most of the trains caught over the next few days were short-formed stopping services, and the resultant exhaust emissions from the myriad types of locomotives working them when starting away from station stops ricocheted, to our delight, noisily back from the wooded slopes through which these trains ran. There was no exact plan – we went where the next 'new' engine took us. If, as occasionally happened, the odd V100 diesel turned up then, unless no alternative was available without stranding us for some time, we would avoid that particular train. Four of the six types we travelled with on that rover ticket were caught in that first day. In order of age they were: Class 38 (1906-1922) 4-6-0s; Class 64 (1926-1940) 2-6-2Ts; Class 50 (1939- 1948) 2-10-0s; and the youngsters, Class 23 (1950- 1959) 2-6-2s. A few services that run along these two routes from Heidelberg to Heilbronn were extended, during the rush hours, to/from the unattractive industrial city of Mannheim. For purely novelty purposes (they run under the wires for the 10½ miles involved) we covered them on that first day. An intensive blitz on the rush hour services that evening alongside the River Neckar, hopping on and off services in both directions and staying on the trains for only one or two stops, was, from a basher's point of view, sheer heaven! After a hot and sunny day the evening breeze and cooling of the air was also most welcome whilst waiting at all those small intermediate stations. Located between these two routes there was a 23-mile branch from Meckesheim to Obrigheim which had one eastbound non-railcar train each day – although, bizarrely, several in the opposite direction. Needless to say, as it turned up with 50.1188, we travelled on it. At the 'terminus' we caught a DB bus to Neckarelz, the line's original destination when it was a through-line. The reason for the road replacement was that the rail bridge over the River Neckar had been damaged some three years previously by river craft and, like our own Severn Bridge, had never been repaired – the entire branch having since been closed. And so, with the steam services ceasing for the night, we headed south from Neckarelz to Stuttgart, the capital city of the federal state we were to travel in for most of the next three days – Baden Wurttemberg. On the journey to our 'beds', we reviewed the day's haulages – 15 runs with 12 different locomotives from four classes totalling 247 miles. It could only get better!

Stuttgart Hauptbahnhof became very familiar to us because, over the next four nights, a great deal of time was spent there! This first occasion, on the Friday morning, we arrived at 00:21 and, having located the carriages which were to form our 04:38 departure for Heilbronn, boarded the darkened, unheated coaches, pulled the blinds down, took our shoes off and settled down in our first-class compartment. Occasionally we were disturbed by either station staff or the local 'polizei' who, thinking they were about to evict some vagrants, threw open the door, blinding us with torchlight, shouting and gesticulating – only to slink away with their tails between their legs when we produced our valid travel tickets! The lack of heat was not a problem because, as luck would have it, we were in the middle of a mini heatwave and the temperature at night was 'pleasantly warm'. Often, our having settled down after one or more of those interruptions, the lights came on (the electric locomotive having coupled up) and we were away, at 04:38, back into travelling mode – awake or not. Upon arriving at Heilbronn Hauptbahnhof, this train had a 22-minute station stop during which a traction change to steam took place. We alighted there and caught a local starting service to the next station, Heilbronn Sulmertor, rejoining the Stuttgart service again following behind to the next station – the aptly named Neckarsulm (where the rivers Neckar and Sulm converge).

Returning to the main Heilbronn station by the same method, we obtained runs with four different locomotives in 44 minutes (06:01 – 06:45). Perhaps it *was* going to get better than yesterday, after all!

Steam was everywhere – on both freight and passenger – with Classes 23, 38, 50 and 64 predominating. More new track beckoned and, with 50.1256 at the front, a 44¾ mile jaunt to the historic city of Karlsruhe was undertaken. This city became home to a large Jewish population attracted by the 16th century founder's offering of incentives without discrimination – thus enticing them to settle there. The Jewish population, regrettably, fell from over 3,000 in 1933 to 18 in 1945 – caused by the Nazis' ethnic cleansing policies. We saw none of the town's attractions because a mere 22 minutes later we were heading back to Heilbronn, albeit with a combination of a Class 38 and a V100 diesel locomotive – in all probability, a balancing move for the diesel. Just 6¾ miles north of Heilbronn was the junction station of Bad Friedrichshall Jagstfeld. The two routes from Heidelberg and a third from Osterburken met here and, with a great number of steam services calling there, was often visited. The length of name soon became a pain to write down and was quickly abbreviated to Bad FJ in the notebook! The less wooded, more open countryside to the east of the area was then passed through en route to our next destination – Crailsheim, where a wonderful steam-saturated vista awaited us. Altogether we reckoned up to 95% of all services were steam operated – the drawback being long gaps between 'mini rush hours' (when several trains departed in quick succession) in respect of frequency. The Class 78 4-6-4Ts (1912) were encountered there for the first time. After travelling the 23 miles south to Aalen, the rest of the day was spent between there and Scorndorf – the changeover station from where Stuttgart bound services were electrically hauled. Similarly to the previous evening, we hopped on and off steam trains at will – including an unusually routed 'express' from Munchen. Instead of travelling direct on the electrically operated main line via Ulm, this train, from Munchen to Stuttgart, meandered cross-country, taking twice as long, via Donaworth and Aalen. Noting the rarity of steam track it covered, some of which our rover ticket did not cater for, we vowed to return for it in the future – in reality three months later. Although the 78s predominated (we caught two consecutively numbered examples on two consecutive services), some Class 50s, seemingly used at random anywhere and everywhere, were also in circulation. To repeat, but with amendments, a paragraph from the previous day's detail – on the journey to our 'bed' that night, we reviewed the day's haulages – 19 runs with 19 different locomotives from five classes totalling 264 miles – it DID get better! Bearing in mind it was only 22:34, our beds for the night – the stock for the following morning's 04:38 departure at Stuttgart – had not yet arrived so a two-hours-each-way 'fill in' trip was made to Mannheim (visiting there from 01:16 to 02:32!) before climbing into our regular overnight accomodation.

Most services throughout mainland Europe, certainly in the sixties, ran seven days per week; therefore, having arrived once again at Heilbronn on the 04:38 from Stuttgart, we were able to repeat the 'four locos in an hour' scenario between there and Neckarsulm similar to yesterday – even though it was a Saturday morning. The final new class of locomotive of the trip, a Class 44 2-10-0, was then caught working down the Crailsheim line on an all-stations service. We were able at one point en route to catch the train it was looped for, to get ahead and photograph it arriving at Schwabisch Hall Hessental (aren't some German stations a mouthful?) before rejoining her. 23.105, the very last steam locomotive built for DB (1959) took us in the first rain – albeit just a shower – during our visit, to the most northerly point of our rover ticket – Lauda. Returning south whilst changing trains at Konigshofen, en route to Osterburken (a lot of new track today), a very helpful railway employee directed us across the tracks to the best position for photography, even pointing out which lines the expected trains would be arriving on. Further help from railway personnel, resulting in a delay to the train itself, was freely given at Bad FJ later in the day when, having alighted from the train, I realised I had mislaid my 'little red notebook'. Jumping back on the train we (Bill, the ticket collector and guard) performed a frantic search resulting in its being found under the seat I had been sitting on. It must be hereditary – my daughter tells me these days – when I attempt to chastise her for doing similarly, albeit with either her train ticket or iPod en route to/from her college! Unusually completing the day's activities at Heidelberg, rather than Stuttgart, that day's tally read 16 runs with 13 different locomotives from five classes totalling 231¼ miles – slightly down from yesterday's 'peak'.

Heidelberg did not have stock berthed overnight in the platforms so a tiresome long wait ensued in the early hours of Sunday morning before being able to catch the 01:28 departure to Stuttgart – for our 'beds'. For this morning and next day (it was a Bank Holiday) we didn't catch the usual 04:38 departure out of Stuttgart (perhaps not running?), the alternative being a later E train and our tickets not being valid in first class! Sacrilege! That Sunday, with slightly reduced services available to us, we concentrated on finishing off the sections of track that our rover allowed us to travel over but had yet to visit. These were the 18½ miles from Neckarelz to Osterburken and the 26 miles from Schwabisch Hall Hessental to Backnang. Throughout the Sunday we were now, having been in the area for three days, coming across the same locomotives – in particular, those of classes 23 and 38. The statistics therefore reflected that fact – still a creditable 14 runs with 13 different locomotives from four classes totalling 248½ miles. Upon arriving back into Stuttgart at the somewhat early time of 22:18, nothing had been berthed up for the night and so a two hour trip each way to Mannheim was again undertaken – with us finally stretching out on the 05:28 stock merely an hour before departure.

Bank Holiday Monday was to be the final day and, as if to complete a full circle of our visit, we ended up on the very train we started our voyage of discovery on four days previously – the 09:06 Heidelberg to Heilbronn, with the very same locomotive – 038.273-9. Having assumed we had caught all the ex-Prussian P8s in circulation, it was a pleasant surprise when a 'new' one, double-headed with an 'old' 50, turned up on our final steam journey on the Heidelberg service in the early afternoon. We then made our way to Saarbrucken, calling in at Kaiserslautern on the off-chance that the small allocation of steam there might produce something. You get extremes of joy or disappointment when attempting to find steam services in areas not previously either reported on or visited by fellow enthusiasts. This occasion, luckily, was one of joy because the 16:22 to Pirmasens, shown in the timetable as railcar, was formed of three coaches and a 'tender first' Class 23! During the turnaround at Pirmasens, 23.028 fetched a further coach from the sidings and the reason for the 'strengthened' train became clear. It was the Bank Holiday and the train was besieged with returning day trippers – having presumably enjoyed the day in this multicultural city in the Federal State of Rheinland Palatinate. Then to Saarbruken where, having checked out one possible steam working to find it was diesel, we went out on the town. 'A big nosh up' is how it was described in my notebook – followed by numerous visits to various bars, some of which, often located in somewhat dubious surroundings, were eye openers. I was, after all, only 21 years old and had led a sheltered life as far as women were concerned!

Returning to the station by four a.m., and because the French rail strike was *still* on, there were no SNCF-operated railcars or 141R workings on the Sarreguemines line. The replacement traction for the 04:09 departure to Hannweiler was in the form of double-headed Class 50s – what a result. Returning to Saarbrucken, we then caught the diverted *Basle Oostende Express* which departed at 05:31 with a German Pacific (01.073) working the train over the border into Luxembourg at Wasserbillig. It still puzzles me, when writing this, as to how we knew that a train normally routed via Strasbourg and Metz would call at Saarbrucken – and, more significantly, be steam powered into a country long since devoid of it. This being our sixth night, and not having slept between clean sheets, we were too tired to care about the whys and wherefores and just sat back or slept the long journey to Oostende – arriving there at 14:30 (246 minutes late). Aboard the *Roi Leopold III*, which departed an hour late after awaiting an international train connection, the full facts of the last few days were gone through – over 1,200 steam miles with 46 new engines from eight classes. It was a joy going over it for this book – an extremely successful excursion into West German steam areas.

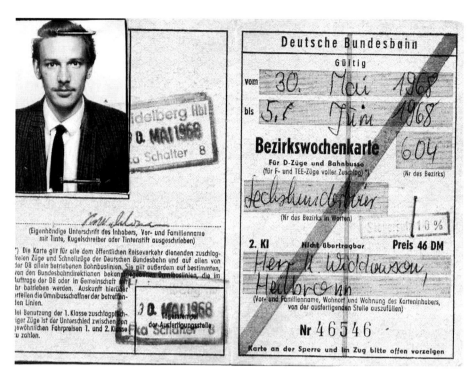

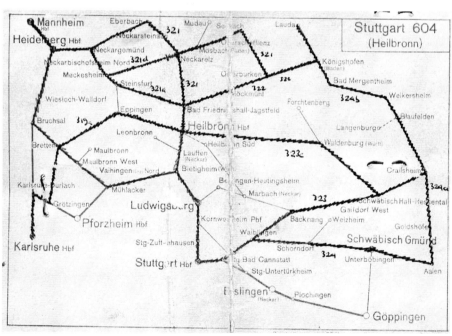

7.01 Class 65 2-8-4T No 002 is seen at Furth after arrival with the 0606 from Weinheim on Thursday 30th May. Fortune shone upon us that day for two reasons. Firstly there were only 18 of these machines built and secondly, with most of the services along this 10½ mile branch shown to be either bus or railcar, we were lucky that this was steam at all!

7.02   6¾ miles north of Heilbronn was the equivalent of Waterloo's Clapham Junction – Bad Friedrichshall Jagstfeld. This station was visited many times and quickly became abbreviated to Bad FJ in our notebooks because it was the junction for two routes from Heidelberg and one from Osterburken thus it was awash with steam operated services. 2-6-2 023.062-3 is seen arriving on the 1148 Stuttgart to Heidelberg train – which she had taken over at Heilbronn.

7.03   Crailsheim was perhaps the best centre for steam in the area with approximately 95% of the local services in the hands of several different classes of steam locomotives. Whilst there were large gaps in between trains these were compensated by 'mini rush hours' of connecting services. One such occasion is seen here on Friday 31st May with 2-10-0 50.1028 and 4-6-4T 78.355 on the 1430 to Aalen and 4-6-0 038.499-0 (nearest camera) ready to depart with the 1419 to Heilbronn.

7.04 Crailsheim and the first rain shower of the trip seems to clean everything up. Here 23.105, the very last steam locomotive built for DB 9 years earlier, readies for departure on Saturday 1st June with the 0921 Ulm to Lauda.

7.05   Probably an engine balancing move the 1246 Heidelberg to Heilbronn was a surprise double header on Bank Holiday Monday 3rd June. About to depart Sinsheim 50.227 and 038.095-6 await 'right away'.

7.06   Friday 31st May at Aalen and 2-6-4T 78.355 prepares to depart with the 1607 to
       Crailsheim. We had arrived behind her a mere 45 minutes earlier from Crailshem when
       she was coupled with 50.1028 and being a tank locomotive we failed to understand why
       she was turned during that short time.

CHAPTER EIGHT

THE HIGHS AND LOWS OF A FRENCH TANK HUNT

08

O N THIS TRIP WE WENT 'TANK HUNTING' and the 'high' was successfully catching the Lille – allocated 242TAs just weeks BEFORE their services were dieselised – the 'low' being missing the 141TAs just weeks AFTER their withdrawal! The extremes of terrain where the two classes 'lived' were very different. The 242TAs were to be found in the flatlands of Northern France, adjacent to the Belgian border, whilst the latter type were in the mountainous scenic Massif Central area – a volcanic plateau in South Central France. Resulting from a union-inspired work-to-rule, which was causing disruption and cancellations to train services throughout Kent, Bill and I decided to travel to Dover on an earlier than normal stopping train out of Charing Cross. In the final event, the 'Night Ferry' did run, albeit with EMU (Electric Multiple Unit) stock – causing sleeping car passengers to finally get their 'through' berths at Dunkerque at 04:30 the following morning! After a rough crossing on the *Shepperton Ferry*, we arrived at Lille at 06:15 in the morning on the last Saturday of June. Noting 141Rs on Seclin and Boulogne trains, we ignored them and deliberately homed in on the 242TA workings from there to Tourcoiny – the border station with Belgium a mere eight miles distant. This 'emergency' trip, based on grapevine information, alerted us to the fact that dieselisation of these services was a mere two weeks hence and with this being the last stronghold of the 242TAs, the class would thus become extinct. There were six tanks in circulation that morning and by making three return trips along the route we caught five of them. One particular train was a pilgrim/hospital special from Lourdes to Tourcoiny. Preceding it out of Lille on a normal service, we alighted at the intermediate station of Roubaix in the hope that the special would call there as well. Not only did it call there but eight of its 18 coaches were detached upon arrival within an admirable ten minutes station stop.

Having achieved our mission there, we headed for our next objective – the 141TAs at Le Mont-Dore. This holiday centre for both skiing and mountaineering enthusiasts was located a few miles east of Clermont Ferrand which, our having 'nearly' reached earlier in the year, was on the still steam-infested Bourbonnais line via Nevers. So we endured the 160 boring electric-hauled miles from Lille to Paris passing through unspectacular countryside, now so quickly accomplished courtesy of the Eurostar services. When destined for the Nevers route earlier that year we, always on the lookout for steam sightings, had noted a 141R on a passenger service at Montargis some 30 miles south of Moret Les Sablons. Careful investigation of the timetable revealed that it was the 18:07 from Paris Lyon service via a secondary route which, my being unable to trace it on present SNCF system maps, has, I believe, subsequently closed. We therefore caught that service that day, disappointedly leaving with a diesel. Nothing ventured, nothing gained, or so we thought, but then at Corbeil Essonnes, a mere 20 miles into our journey, it was exchanged for a Nevers allocated 141R 554. A delightful 57 ¾-mile ride on a sunlit evening was then enjoyed over this predominately DMU (Diesel Multiple Unit) operated line. I believe we were the first English 'gricers' (one of many derogatory names awarded to railway enthusiasts by non-followers of our hobby) to have discovered this train – which made it even more appreciated! A 12 minute connection into the 18:57 ex-Paris reaped my first dud (already caught before!) 241P – giving way to its 'required' sister 24 at Nevers. Yet again we didn't reach the train's destination of Clermont Ferrand, the capital of Auvergne province, deliberately alighting at St Germain des Fosses at 23:07 for the plethora of summer only/dated services which, it being the first week of the holiday season, had commenced running that weekend.

It always seemed to me as though the majority of the French train-travelling public, certainly in those days, had a propensity to undertake long-distance journeys at night. Lengthy (compared with Britain) trains criss-crossed France in the early hours – often crowded to the point of standing room only, none more so than was witnessed on that last Sunday in June. Luckily for us, SNCF had yet to supply sufficient diesels in the area to cope with the seasonal extras and upon completion of a mini bash – at 07:45 in the morning at Clermont-Ferrand – runs with four 141Rs had been entered into our notebooks. The night was warm and humid, and waiting at the various stations on the main line was a pleasant break from the conditions on the trains caught. Jumping on and off these 141R-hauled services, at unearthly times in the twilight hours, in this steam-infested area, perhaps the most unexpected catch was oil-fired 141R1108. She was working a mere 14¼ miles from Gannet to St Germain des Fosses on the 22:16 from Bordeaux to Geneve which, by 6:30 in the morning, still had some distance to complete the marathon journey from the Atlantic coast to the Swiss lakeside. Any through passengers certainly deserved medals for endurance!

Now to find those elusive 141TAs! Departing Clermont Ferrand and setting off into the hills on an aging railcar, the signs, when changing at the junction station of Laqueville, were not encouraging. The eight-mile branch from there to Le Mont-Dore, the spa town centre for skiers and mountaineers on this volcanic plateau and so frequented by tourists, was scenically pleasant enough – but steamless. All services were in the hands of railcars or diesel locomotives, two more of which we caught to Ussel, the last outpost in our quest to find these seemingly elusive tanks. We were two weeks too late! The Shedmaster, perhaps sensing our disappointment, allowed us to wander at will around the lines of withdrawn steam locomotives at the shed. Although a 141F (my only sighting of that particular class) arrived, whilst we were there, on freight, and several 141TAs were in light steam, there were, according to him, no booked steam passenger services remaining. Sixteen of these tanks were in the derelict state of storage together with the third type of French steam I had never seen before – a 230G. The temperature was by now in the high 40s centigrade and so two thoroughly sweaty, tired (after two nights' travelling) dejected enthusiasts departed on the 14:20 to Paris d'Austerlitz – yet another new capital terminal to me. After crossing Paris, we caught the 22:00 'Night Ferry' via Dunkerque, the *Saint Germain* and the EMU operated (the work-to-rule still preventing the through wagon-lits to run) service to London. As always in any travels into untapped territory, some you win, some you lose. The next few weeks were the last of any British steam activity and European steam chasing was put on hold.

8.01   Croix Wasquehal, an intermediate station on the Lille to Belgian border station of Tourcoing, and the author is caught in his travelling garb – we all wore ties in those days! These 4-8-4T 242TA tanks were to be displaced by diesels two weeks later – No 105 seen arriving with the 1302 Tourcoing to Paris Nord on Saturday 29th June. This photograph was given to me by Bill at our one and only meeting in preparation for this book – his untimely death 3 months later preventing any further photographic content being supplied by him.

8.02   It was 0630 on Sunday 30th June and this overnight cross country service, the 2216
        Bordeaux to Geneve, had only reached Gannet where, upon reversal oil-fired 2-8-2 141R
        1108 was to take the service a mere 14 miles to St Etienne – handing over to an electric
        locomotive. Any through passengers surely qualified for an endurance medal!

8.03   In temperatures of over 40 degrees centigrade, 2-8-2 141F 189 simmers on shed at Ussel
        having arrived on a freight train on Sunday 30th June. This was the only sighting of a
        member of that class – and indeed was the only steam activity, most services having been
        dieselised just two weeks previously.

8.04   Missed by two weeks. 2-8-2T 141TAs rest and rust at the back of Ussel shed on Sunday
        30th June. (310/347/336/441/322/486)

8.05   This is Lille in pre Eurostar and TGV days. The 0730 Paris Nord to Tourcoing, having arrived with an electric locomotive from the capital, is about to be taken forward for the remaining 13 kilometres by 4-8-4T 242TA102 – Saturday 29th June.

THE TITLE OF THIS CHAPTER REFERS TO my foray to the uncharted, to me, territories in Western France – the Atlantic coast. Nothing ever being straightforward, the overnight accommodation for the first night was to become my last visit down the Bourbonnais line. Oh, how I wanted runs with those 241Ps! The Channel crossing on this last Friday in August was on the *Maid of Orleans* and was smooth enough for us (John, Deno and me) to enjoy what was perhaps our last hot meal for several days. This crossing was, unusually for me, to Boulogne, and that day's slow crawl through the docks complex was undertaken by the home depot's 141R587. A rain-soaked crossing of Paris at the height of the rush hour was endured on the Metro before catching the 18:07 secondary-routed train to Montargis from the Lyon station. Changing there onto the 18:57 'main line' train, the 'dud' 241P was exchanged for a required one at Nevers. Train 1109 has been documented as the most arduous assignment remaining for French steam power – 600 tons to Nevers where three coaches were detached. Skimming through past issues of *Railway World*, I came across an article by M. T. Hedderly (Sept. '70) who actually rode on the footplate of this very train. His three-page description of the train's performance, together with a precise log of the run, highlighted the skill of the driver in ensuring this heavy train maintained the schedule (See Appendix I). Alighting at St Germain des Fosses to catch what was in circulation, we began to appreciate that the 68xxx diesels were making inroads into what had previously guaranteed Mountain-hauled trains. A combination of that fact and of poor timekeeping on trains in the up direction caused us to chance upon a Lyon Perrache to Le Mans cross-country service – operated by a 141R from St Germain to Vierzon. Taking her the short distance to Moulins, we changed, at 02:25 in the morning (it HAD to be done!), onto what was, retrospectively, my final required Nevers-allocated 241P on a following Paris bound service. All my runs with the Nevers Mountains were during the hours of darkness so not only did I miss the apparently scenic Loire valley countryside through which they passed but was unable to obtain photographs of it – my camera not being equipped with any flash attachment. Subsequent research revealed that at the beginning of the year Nevers had ten 241Ps – whittled down to seven by the time of this visit – with a further three being withdrawn the following month. The large 72000 diesel locomotives arrived in the area in January '69 resulting in a single 241P, No 7, being retained as a standby. To obtain runs with all the survivors available was a most satisfactory outcome – albeit not realised at the time!

Crossing over to my sixth new Paris terminus, Montparnasse, my planned blitz of the Ouest region's steam services commenced. All these trips/journeys throughout Europe were made after hours spent studying timetables, in the evenings/days now bereft of British steam chasing, and were used as a basic plan – usually being adhered to. Sometimes, however, 'emergency' variations had to be encompassed resulting from unexpected steam workings or diesel substitutions. It was the Bank Holiday Saturday morning at Montparnasse and two departures – the 08:00 to the popular seaside resort of Granville and the 08:33 to Argentan – were in the hands of 141Ps 150 and 200 respectively. The only passenger services this class was rostered to by that date were summer dated and relief services on this route and, to obtain runs with both these locomotives, a change en route at Dreaux was made. Alighting from the second train at Argentan, an apparent axis of the line, at 11:30, and with no steam passenger activity scheduled for the next three hours, a return diesel trip was made to the junction station of Mezidon (on the Cherbourg line) to view the nearby steam cemetery. My two colleagues failed to make the return train because the dump was too large to undertake a complete 'survey' in the 68-minute turnaround the train had, and so I returned to Argentan alone. A further study of the timetable revealed that by travelling the 28 miles east along the Granville branch to Flers, I was able to return on a service booked to run on a mere five occasions, only, that year – the 14:06 Granville to Paris. Although this was a prime candidate for steam haulage, until the telltale wisp of smoke and plaintive whistle indicated success, nothing was taken for granted. 141P115 duly arrived with a standing-room-only availability of space to be had – not even room to make an entry in my notebook – until alighting again at Argentan some 33 minutes later. The next two hours were spent observing the busy freight scene which was predominantly 141Rs, the 141Ps (with only weeks to live) being seemingly restricted to passenger services, before travelling to the racing circuit town of Le Mans. Having already visited both the Est and Sud-Ouest allocations of 241Ps, this final pocket of twelve 241Ps awaited me. Before the night reliefs and extras, on which these locomotives were expected, I noticed the 20:02 departure for Tours had 141R68 in charge. Quick reference to the timetable confirmed that I was able to travel on this train, over the normally railcar-worked line, returning three hours later into Le Mans – well in time for the first Mountain of the visit, No 13, working a Paris to Quimper service.

Having deliberately alighted at Angers at 01:30 – to catch a following Mountain-hauled service – fatigue took over and I fell asleep on a wooden bench – later finding out that I missed two steam reliefs heading for Nantes! Suitably refreshed after the three hour kip, I boarded the first available train to Nantes – annoyingly worked by a diesel! Arriving there at 05:56, I ran and jumped aboard a 141R hauled service leaving from the opposite platform – subsequently turning out to be the 05:55 departure (luckily departing two minutes late) to Quimper. Both my colleagues (last seen at Mezidon the previous day) were already on the train and, having given me up for lost, had eaten my allocation of pears jointly purchased earlier in the trip! This Nantes-based, oil-fired 141R took us on a glorious Sunday morning ride along the Atlantic coast to Brittany's oldest city – Quimper. The French railwaymen had taken these American Mikados to their hearts. They were reliable, versatile and trusted for any type of work by both crews and shed staff alike, and although often rough-riding, the large roomy cab environment was presumably a compensating factor. With the weather, this Sunday morning, having started off with a series of rain storms and becoming a splendidly sunny day, I would have thought the crew would have enjoyed the 158-mile journey as much as we did. Having ascertained, after arrival at 09:30, that the next steam going anywhere was the return working at 19:10, a fill-in trip to Brest was made. There, four 141Rs were in steam on shed but all extras were in the hands of diesels. The 15:38 return to Quimper was an interesting train, albeit diesel. It was formed of BB66234, one van, two six wheeled coaches, one van, three coaches (locked) and five assorted freight wagons – a very mixed train which shunted the sidings en route at Chateaulin!

Arriving back at Nantes Orleans, which somewhat resembled London's Euston station (which, during 1968, was undergoing rebuilding in connection with the WCML electrification and was, in effect, a building site with workmen's huts for ticket offices and restaurants), the third and final day in the area started with a return trip in the early hours to/from Angers with 241Ps 16 and 32 – and this time managing to stay awake for the 1½-hour wait in the early hours. Then, what a choice! It was either the subsequently-preserved 231G558 on the 05:57 to Les Sablons or 231D648 on the 06:28 to St Nazaire (which was booked for a 141R) – finally deciding on the 06:28 because it was a new class to me. At Montoir de Bretagne we crossed with the first train out of Le Croisic which had 141C81 as its motive power and was another class that I had hoped to catch, this area being their last outpost. The result was a rapid evacuation onto the service, which caused me to severely knock my elbow on the handrail when jumping down to the platform. This made my arm very painful and it remained bruised and somewhat numb for several days, almost leading me to abandon the week-long bash in West Germany I had planned. The train terminated at Savenay, en route passing 231D589 on empty coaching stock heading for Le Croisic. In the hope that she was to return promptly with a passenger service, we travelled to the Atlantic coast resort for what turned out to be an 11:14 (relief) to Paris, worked by her to Nantes and taken forward by 241P30 whose grimy condition contrasted sharply with the 231D. All the Nantes former Etat Pacifics were withdrawn within days! Changing one last time at Angers for a following service (booked diesel!) worked by sister No 27, I finally left the Ouest area after successful collecting over 900 steam miles with 14 locomotives from five classes. Ominously, 72002, a prototype diesel locomotive reputedly as powerful as France's currently most powerful unit, the 241P, was noted working on several occasions with various trains. I now headed alone into Paris where, as tradition dictated, having four hours to kill before my 22:35 departure out of the Lyon station, a return trip to St Denis for more 141TCs was undertaken.

Tuesday morning saw me meeting Bill, with whom the next few days would be spent touring West Germany, at the prearranged time of 04:30 at Belfort. Taking advantage of continued steam passenger services in the area, two further runs with 141Rs were undertaken before catching the two-coach 07:44 Mulhouse to Freiburg cross-border (over the Rhein) service. In a replication of the nearby Delle border crossing earlier this year, it seemed that the SNCF gave little importance to such services – providing, in this instance, a tender-first, run-down 141R369 'wheezing like the sound of an injured seagull' (quote from notebook) for the 11¾ miles to Neuenburg – the border station. As with the aforementioned Delle service, it was taken forward by the receiving country's electric locomotive – a marked contrast to SNCF's provision of power. The route, not surprisingly, is now freight-only.

9.01   The Atlantic coast resort of Granville had numerous extra summer relief trains on the route from Paris and it was this type of work that the remaining 2-8-2 141P's were utilised on. Here, at the head of the 0800 departure from Paris Montparnasse, is 141P150 on Bank Holiday Saturday 31st August. Within weeks, at the cessation of the summer dated trains, the entire class was withdrawn.

9.02   One of a handful of survivors of the 2-8-2 class 141C181 after arrival at Savanay with the
       0651 from Le Croisic on Bank Holiday Monday 2nd September. It was whilst alighting
       from this train, in a rush to obtain this photograph, that I severely 'damaged' my arm and
       put in doubt a planned week long visit to West Germany – but I soldiered on!

71

9.03   Having passed her earlier that day heading for Le Croisic with an empty stock service, we backtracked to the Atlantic coast resort to ascertain what she was going to work. We would have waited all day but luckily within a couple of hours she was to work on 1114 additional service to Paris on that Bank Holiday Monday 2nd September. Here seen reposing in the sidings is 4-6-2 231D589 – again one of the few survivors of the class. We were indeed fortunate with our catches that Bank Holiday.

9.04   In pre Eurotunnel days this would have been the starting point for many holidaymakers
        bound for far away places. Posing at Boulogne Maritime on Friday 30th August is 2-8-2
        141R587 on the 1318 Relief to Paris Nord. The first part of the journey, through the docks
        complex, would be preceded by a flag waving, whistle-blowing official whose job was
        to ensure safe passage by making parked cars and pedestrians hopefully move out of the
        way.

CHAPTER TEN

FROM THE LAKES TO THE FORESTS AND BACK

10

S O OFF WE WENT, ON MY THIRD visit to West Germany in search of steam. Rhein, Hamburg and the northern part of this country were expected to remain a steam area for several years, so I did not make it a priority to visit. All the exploits that my friends and colleagues experienced with Pacifics on services to Emden and Norrdeich having vowed to 'get there someday' – were, sadly, missed by myself. Whilst appreciating that I lost out on the final main line steam activity in Europe (which finally died off in 1977), I can only relate here that which I *did* witness – for which I am truly appreciative.

On this first Tuesday in September, having crossed into West Germany from France, we made our way to the Swiss city of Basle. Our eventual destination was Lake Konstanz where it was possible that a small allocation of Class 50s perhaps worked some services in the area. No other enthusiast colleagues had been this way to report any steam passenger activity and it was on a wing and a prayer that we ventured into the unknown. Our connection forward to Lake Konstanz gave us three hours that morning to tour the cafes and streets adjacent to the German station of Basle Badischer. Unaware that ANY steam services ran in Switzerland, to say we were surprised was an understatement when we passed what turned out to be the 13:16 Waldshut to Basle – with 50.2838! With hopes raised for possible success, they materialised in the catching of three Class 50s on local services in the Konstanz area! The blisteringly hot sunshine, together with beautiful lakeside scenery and the knowledge that we had tapped into previously unreported steam trains, meant that, whilst the mileages were not high, we were! At Singen, an unattractive industrial town located near the extinct Hohentweil volcano, we walked to the shed, noting some stored Class 94 tanks, in an attempt to find out about any further steam workings in the area. The language barrier however proved insurmountable and, none the wiser, we returned to the station where, whilst supping some soup and contemplating our next moves, some serious thunder and lightning heralded the end of the hot spell. Deciding that no benefit would be gained by staying out all night, we travelled the short distance to Radolfzell and found a B. & B. for the night, for DM8 (£0.85).

Up early on the Wednesday, we 'hit' the morning rush hour services only to catch just one further Class 50 – albeit a new locomotive. Some time was lost whilst waiting around in the hope of further steam haulage but by mid-morning we called it a day and headed north to a known pocket of Class 38s – at Tuttlingen. From here to Rottweil, Horb and Tubingen, the line ran via the Neckar Valley and was particularly scenic – through which these 60-year-old Prussian P8s ensured that all and sundry knew they were coming with their exhausts echoing off the surrounding, steeply-wooded hillsides. None of the five locomotives caught during our day-long bash of the services had been included in the computer renumbering which DB was currently undertaking – was their end too close to bother with? The weather had now changed into continuous rain with occasional cloudy breaks and, coming across a V100 diesel service, the opportunity to dry out in the station buffet at Sulz over a bowl of soup (with a whole egg yolk floating in it!) was taken. We eventually left the area on the 17:53 from Horb – which was one of the few steam-hauled services to Tubingen from where electric traction took over for the 45 remaining miles to Stuttgart. Before we boarded that train, however, taking into consideration we were starving, a visit to a local supermarket enabled us to dine like kings on the Stuttgart-bound train. Starting with a bar of chocolate, the main course was bread and butter with jam, followed by some chocolate sponge, assorted broken biscuits (a bargain at under DM2), an orange, more chocolate and finishing off with a smoke. Two points come to mind – first, the heavy dependence on chocolate and second, what on earth possessed me to write all this down? Makes a change from just a boring list of haulages, I suppose. I wasn't feeling all that well at this point because not only was my damaged arm giving a lot of gip but a streaming cold and a stye in my eye were not helping my demeanour! A six-minute connection at Stuttgart saw us head for Wurzberg en route (albeit, in the hope of steam, via secondary lines) to the guaranteed Pacific-infested routes centred on the Bavarian town of Hof. Arriving at Wurzburg, courtesy of my longest steam ride within West Germany – 79 miles – at 22:18, we decided to stay out overnight so as to catch some pre-dawn trains in the area which could be steam. Still hungry after our 'feast' some five hours earlier, chicken and chips were enjoyed in what could best be described as the German equivalent of a Lyons Corner House.

Returning to the station, we boarded what we thought was the 00:33 to Gemunden, a mere 27 miles distant, only to eventually realise that it was the 00:28 *Karnten Express* which, although going *via* Gemunden, had as its first calling point the East German border town of Bebra – 83 miles further. An easy mistake to make, we told ourselves – both trains being in adjacent platforms – and, having viewed a DR (Deutsche Reichsbahn – East Germany Railways) Class 01.5, we returned on the southbound *Karnten Express* alighting at Gemunden at 04:52 on this Thursday morning. Strange that the northbound didn't call there but the southbound did – but it filled the night up and eliminated long waits at stations. The only non-railcar train of the day, over a secondary route from Gemunden to Schweinfurt, was the 05:18 departure – which rewarded us with yet another run with one of the ubiquitous Class 50 locomotives. We chanced on the possibility of steam on a Mellrichstadt branch service by travelling out from Schweinfurt a mere six miles to Poppenhausen to catch it back in – resulting in a run with a Class 78 tank. It seemed that most branch lines had just one loco-hauled service each, usually very early morning, which usually produced steam traction. Daylight, of sorts, was now breaking, it being cloudy and dull as we made our way to Coburg. Here was an allocation of the 1928-built Class 86 tank locomotives, to me yet another new class, which might be working passenger services over branch lines in the area. A visit to the shed resulted in a very helpful depot master who luckily had a smattering of English and provided us with a 'spare' copy of the relevant locomotive duties. You've guessed it – they only worked very early awkward services or, more interestingly, several evening 'rush hour' services. As, by now, it was only mid-morning, we decided to return for the latter services the following evening and made our way to Lichtenfels – the traction-changing location on the Nurnberg to Hof route. The retention of steam power for train services in the Hof area indirectly resulted from the political upheaval after World War II. Once an important railway junction, Hof was strategically located at the convergence of main lines from Nurnberg and Munchen to Berlin, Leipzig and Dresden. With the creation of the Iron Curtain 'allocating' Bavaria to the West and Saxony to the East, though, train travel opportunities were discouraged, leaving Hof effectively at the end of a 'stub'. Electrification, so favoured throughout West Germany for main lines, was not therefore considered viable for such an insignificant traffic flow – thankfully allowing, from an enthusiast's perspective, the retention of steam power. It was not just the splendid forestry scenery that was so delightful about this 58-mile main line but also the switchback route the line had to take through the hilly terrain. Some sharp gradients also contributed to either storming climbs or rapid descents – testing the capabilities of the 22 Hof-based Pacifics which, judging by both appearance and performance, were well up to the job. In the early afternoon we saw the English-speaking Station Master at Hof, to whom Bill had previously written, and he indicated (using our DB timetable) which services had 'Dampflok' on them. We spent the remainder of the day covering secondary routes in the area, enjoying runs with a rebuilt 01, a 50 and two 64 tanks, before ending up at Weiden where, having located a hotel, we just managed to make it into our beds before falling asleep.

On the Friday we commuted back into Hof where our original plan was to travel through East Germany to Poland and Czechoslovakia but, resulting from the Warsaw Pact troops' invasion just three weeks prior, the Iron Curtain was closed. Despite having trooped around the London Embassies earlier that year obtaining the necessary visas, the answer was still 'niet'. What were we, then, going to do? Luckily, we had seen an advert at Konstanz earlier in the week which offered a Dampflok train around the lake for the coming Sunday. All we could do was kill time in this corner of West Germany, and having met yesterday's friendly Station Master, a tour of his shed helped alleviate our disappointment. My last shed tour had been at Carnforth on Britain's last day of steam the previous month, the difference being that, here, steam was still living and with a future – albeit just under five years. Departing Hof behind a Class 50, we then spent just under three hours jumping on and off trains at Falls and Munchberg, catching runs with three of Hof's Pacifics before, as we'd promised ourselves yesterday, arriving at Coburg in time for the evening Class 86 – worked services. Coburg, in those days, was surrounded on three sides by the Iron Curtain. Of the three branches worked by these large tanks, two of them, to Neustadt and Rodach, had originally gone through to 'the other side'. Researching the present German railway situation, I discovered that the Neustadt line has been reinstated through to Sonneburg and has indeed been electrified. The third branch, which our schedule did not permit time enough to cover, was to Rossach – and has been subsequently closed. Although the Neustadt train was an out-and-back working, the second branch we covered – to Rodach – wasn't, the stock being put away for the following day's service – and in consequence we had to catch a V80 diesel service back to Coburg. There being no suitable overnight services in the area to sleep on, we stopped that night in a hotel – this time at Bayreuth.

On the Saturday morning we travelled the short distance to Kirchenlaibach to connect into the reportedly steam-worked 07:08 Hof to Nurnberg but, alas, it was a diesel. Plan B swung into action and we were over the moon when the 08:11 Bayreuth to Weiden arrived double-headed with two Class 64s. Our euphoria was short-lived, however, when the required leading tank was taken off, leaving us with her not-required sister! I suppose we should have been grateful it was steam at all. Even the 54-mile scenic run south to Regensburg was behind an 01 already travelled with – we had obviously saturated the area. It was time to move on! At Munchen – famous for its Oktoberfest beer festival at which strong-armed wenches serve several foaming litres of beer to the tables in just one visit (I know because I witnessed it some years later – well worth going to) – we went shopping and bought some bread rolls, postcards and an English newspaper. I had left England eight days previously and you never know – something might have happened of interest back home! We then caught the 14:00 departure to Stuttgart which, the readers might remember, was the train that we had promised ourselves to travel on some three months earlier because of its unusual routing via Donaworth and Aalen. Unbelievably, it was the same Class 78 – no new locomotives that day! Although despondent at not having any new haulages, at least we avoided paying any fares during the trek south via Ulm to Freidrichshafen – necessary to position ourselves in readiness for the steam-hauled rail tour seen advertised earlier that week. The town of Freidrichshafen, whose main claim to fame is that the Zeppelin airship was manufactured there, is located on the north bank of Lake Konstanz and, judging by our inability to find a room for the night, can be very popular with weekenders. We eventually ended up at the 'polizeiwache' (cop shop) hoping for a bed in the cells but they, after several phone calls, unfortunately found us some beds at an exorbitant (not recorded) price.

Sunday morning dawned bright and sunny and a three-minute trip with an inevitable V100 diesel took us from the Stadt (main) station down to the Hafen (harbour). Translating the German description of the tour, it meant 'Around Lake Konstanz with a steam locomotive'. The DM28 (£2.85) tour started from the harbour station, being propelled to the main station and thence to Lindau where 03.222 ran round. On, then, to Bregenz (Austria) where the town band gave us a momentous send-off before proceeding to Lustenau (Austria) and St Margrethen (Switzerland) – both being photo stops. All along the route, in all the countries visited, crowds lined the trackside waving and cheering – it really was a carnival atmosphere. There were more families than enthusiasts aboard and, although documented as being the first main line steam to run in Switzerland for 20 years, I am not so sure of that headline taking into consideration the steam into Basle seen earlier that week. The halfway-round point of the tour was Konstanz itself where all tour participants had ample opportunity to eat, drink or explore the town and, in our case, get some money (no cashpoints then, having to be reliant upon the opening hours of the bureau de change). The old part of the town, south of the River Rhine, is particularly attractive, not having been, if it is to be believed, bombed by Allied forces because the residents, by leaving all the lights on at night, fooled the aircrews into believing it was in neutral Switzerland. The Pacific then hauled us, tender first, to Radolfzell where she ran round, and after eight hours and 108 miles we finally arrived back at Freidrichshafen. A never-to-be-forgotten experience and a fitting finale to my ten day adventure – or so I thought! Lurking in some sidings was an 03 – and it was facing the Ulm direction. Enquiries (from whom?) revealed that she was to work a relief to Stuttgart. After a two-hour wait (we would have waited forever!), 03.281 took us the 64½ miles to Ulm – the final stronghold of the class which eventually survived a further five years. Bill and I then went our separate ways at Ulm, he staying on in West Germany whilst I, running out of annual leave, headed home. Catching the 23:48 *Tauern Express* from Stuttgart, and being excessed en route to the tune of 40 Belgian Francs, I phoned the office upon arrival at Oostende, albeit at 09:29 on the Monday morning, to ask for that very day to be taken as annual leave.

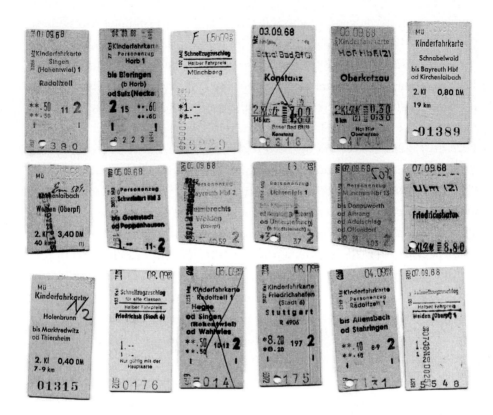

80

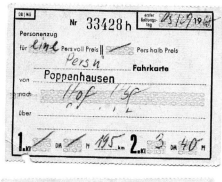

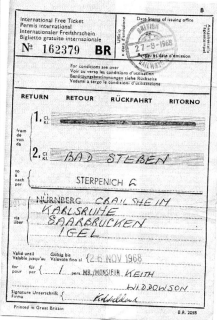

10.01 A few isolated early morning and evening rush hour services in the Coburg area were worked by the small class of 4-6-4T Class 86 locomotives. Having visited the shed at Coburg the previous day the friendly shed master indicated in our public timetable which they were and here, at the end of a 9¼ mile branch, at Rodach is 86.419 having worked the 1726 from Coburg on Friday 6th September.

82

10.02 Having been looped for a faster service to overtake, the driver takes the opportunity for an inspection of his locomotive at Munchberg whilst working the 1126 Litchenfels to Hof on Friday 6th September. 4-6-2 01.202, similar to most of the Hof allocated Pacifics, appears to be in immaculate condition.

10.03 This is Bregenz in Austria on the occasion of the circular steam trip around Lake
Konstanz on Sunday 8th September. Although we were aboard because of the novelty
value of a German steam Pacific locomotive travelling from West Germany via Austria
and Switzerland, we were outnumbered by families enjoying the day out. The town band
was turned out here giving the entire day a wonderful carnival atmosphere.

10.04   A known pocket of ex Prussian P8 locomotives were allocated to Tubingen. With only months to live, therefore DB not bothering to allocate a computer number, 4-6-0 38.1282 sits in the rain at Tuttlingen awaiting departure with the 11.12 to Stuttgart on Wednesday 4th September.

10.05   Lustenau in Austria. The Eurovapour tour around Lake Konstanz on this lovely sunny
day of Sunday 8th September pauses for yet another photographic stop.

CHAPTER ELEVEN

THE PACIFIC DELUGE

11

AVING, BY THE OCTOBER OF '68, PASSED through the Nord (Northern France) region on many occasions, I decided that not enough of my time had been devoted to the steam scene on our doorstep. With rumours circulating regarding the imminent cessation of Calais' Pacifics, I set off, seemingly alone for a change, on Friday 18th October aboard the 22:00 'Night Ferry' out of London Victoria. Upon arrival at Dover Marine, we were advised to remain in the train for a further hour – the inwards working of the *Twickenham Ferry* having been delayed which meant it wouldn't be arriving into Dover until 00:25. The time passed quickly, passengers being entertained by an American girl (from Texas, don't you know!) relating her travelling experiences and, after being allowed aboard, we eventually arrived at Dunkerque over 2½ hours late. Looking at my notes, I had entered 'because of the excessive late running, instead of going to Lille I cut short my itinerary by going direct to Hazebrouck.' I can only assume my original plan was to have gone to Lille for a cross-country journey to Boulogne – with the 141Rs seen there in June – but subsequently never covering that route. I then caught the 09:56 departure to Calais Ville, the first of the two daily steam services over the 40-mile stretch originating from Basle nine hours earlier. After the short hop into the Maritime station with the first of three 231Ks caught that day, I met up with three like-minded colleagues, Mike, Richard and 'Pest' (did anyone know his real name?), with whom I enjoyed an exhilarating run to Boulogne Ville on the *La Fleche D'Or* with the now-preserved 231K8. A max of 73mph was achieved en route , with loose coal from the recently replenished tender showering the first coach – where all enthusiasts naturally congregated on most steam journeys. The following 'semi', usually a 141R, was on this day another Pacific –

the subsequently preserved 231K22. Noting five separate steam departures out of Boulogne (17:43, 18:17, 18:26, 18:35 and 18:38), I thought all this steam so close to home couldn't (and indeed, didn't) last for much longer.Still, 'make hay whilst the sun shines' as the saying goes, and we went on to collect three further 141R runs on either semis or locals before making our way home via the 20:10 *Italia Express* departure from Calais Ville to Hazebrouck en route to Dunkerque Ville. We then had five hours to kill before the 02:30 train ferry departure from Dunkerque Ferry. This time was spent frequenting the numerous bars in the town before walking, or perhaps staggering, the two miles to the ferry – navigating the way through the docks complex by following the silvery railway track which was lit by the moon! I am not sure how many train ferries worked the Dunkerque to Dover route but *Shepperton, Hampton and Twickenham*, together with the French *Saint Germain*, featured many times in my travels. This service went through several locks before the open sea and conveyed through sleeping cars (wagon-lits) from Paris to London (first-class only). Travelling second-class, the nondescripts such as me had to walk on/off the boat at each port but, by boarding the ferry before the train from Paris was due, I had the choice of the best, i.e. corner, bunks. Having purchased a berth in the dormitory sleeping quarters (7/6d – 37p), where, if it was rough, all the curtains surrounding each bunk swayed in synchronicity, I attempted to sleep on (under the pillow) that trip's duty-free allowance. As an aside, by often travelling on the British legs of the 'Night Ferry' and *Golden Arrow* I was able to catch (by default) 19 out of the 24 examples of the Class 71 electric locomotives. As they were used mainly for freight and newspaper trains throughout Kent, I had to resort, during 1969, to viewing the down *Arrow* at Petts Wood Junction and, if it was one of the four remaining 'requirements', travel down to Dover for its return *Arrow* working. My mother was not amused – her day's meal arrangements for me being thrown into disarray. It was, don't forget, in the days before pre-packed frozen meals and microwaves.

11.01 Awaiting the right away at Calais Maritime is one of Calais' magnificent Pacifics – 231K8. The train is the southbound 'Golden Arrow' on Saturday 19th October and although just 12 weeks away from withdrawal, she was one of the lucky ones and now runs as a preserved locomotive throughout France.

Chapter Twelve

More Tanks – But No More Mountains!

12

THIS EXPEDITION COMBINED A SUSTAINED BLITZ ON suburban tanks in the Paris area together with an abortive return visit to the final pocket of 241Ps at Le Mans. The date now was Friday 7th November and, having departed London Victoria once again on the 22:00 'Night Ferry', after a rough crossing on the *Hampton Ferry*, an on-time arrival of 08:40 into Paris Nord set us (Dave and me) up for a seven hour blitz on the 141TC-operated network. The push/pull fitted 141TCs reigned supreme on the remaining non-electrified branches emanating from Gare du Nord. These steam-hauled suburban trains were operated so efficiently with quick turnarounds and impressive speeds between stations that, rather than dieselise the services, steam was kept on until the electrification of the entire system was completed in December 1970. My geographic recollection of the suburban network is now sufficiently rusty to appreciate which of these branches was still steam-operated – looking at my notes from the time, the predominant destinations appear to be Persan Beaumont, Ermont Eaubonne and Epinay Villetaneus, with several engines caught on a cross-country route to Argenteuil. At Persan Beaumont, amongst the now-familiar sight of overhead electric paraphernalia, I noted 231E27 (a type apparently used on the Calais boat trains) and a 050TG – two classes never seen before, or for that matter, again. Any spare time when passing through Gare du Nord, throughout my Paris-routed European adventures, was either spent on a return trip to the first station out (St Denis – four miles) or to a nearby 'British' pub which served Red Barrel bitter – at the time a welcome change from the bottled fizz the French called beer but poor in comparison with the choices of real ale available nowadays throughout Britain! On one occasion I was unwittingly even on a 16:35 St Denys to Gare du Nord (empty coaching stock!), all of which enabled me to eventually obtain runs with 27 different locomotives of the 141TC class. During another visit to the suburban network, disaster occurred when a booking clerk pointed out that the stamp (similar to a postage stamp) had fallen off my International Authority Card – which meant I would have to pay full fare wherever I went during the remaining validity of the card! A trip to the British Rail office in the capital was made and I will always be grateful for the 'personal' sacrifice made by one of the clerks there who peeled off the stamp from her own card for me! Needless to say, when returning home, I Sellotaped it on in case it ever happened again!

After crossing Paris during the height of the rush to the draughty Montparnasse station, a not-particularly-successful return visit to the Nantes area was made in the hope that some of the additional services (it must have been yet another French bank holiday weekend) would provide runs with some of the Ouest allocation of 241Ps not yet caught by me. We changed at Sable off the 18:16 (relief) Paris to Rennes (241P16) onto the booked 18:28 Paris to Nantes (241P13) and, having arrived at 21:20 at Nantes (which was *still* resembling a building site) to find no steam reliefs returning to the capital, killed time in local amusement arcades before returning to the station in time for our 02:13 departure back to Paris. Whilst waiting there we saw 141R1340 arrive, hauling 72003(DL) on a service from Paris – but, regrettably, 72003 was returned to service in time for the very train we were to catch. Just to rub salt into the wound, when leaving Nantes we observed another 141R waiting to work the 21:45 (relief) from Paris forward to Quimper. That was it in respect of the 241Ps, with the Nantes allocation somehow surviving until the end of the summer service the following year on a meagre diet of summer dateds and reliefs. Of the 35 built, only 26 made it into 1968, out of which I caught 13 so I consider myself lucky to have enjoyed 18 runs with them totalling over 1,400 miles. Indeed, the Ouest region itself became steam-free by September 1971.

Returning to Paris on that Saturday morning, a return visit to the Bastille trains reaped runs with four 141TBs (two of which were required) before crossing over to the Nord suburban services for some further runs with the 141TCs before heading homeward on the 14:27 to Calais. This port, back in the late sixties, was merely a large, somewhat down-at-heel, 'resort' on the English Channel. With the opening of the Chunnel, its importance diminished even further until, with borders between European countries effectively withdrawn, it has become known throughout the world as the collecting point for immigrants (political or economic) en route into Britain. Anyway, back to that November day of '68. Whilst noting that 231K30 (one of two Pacifics I failed to catch a run with – the other being 231K44) had failed at Noyelles on the southbound *Arrow* – it subsequently running 90 minutes late with a replacement 141R – our mini bash on Calais locals was unaffected. These remaining Pacifics were nearly 50 years old and, whilst seemingly running like a well-oiled sewing machine, were obviously becoming worn out. After the standard returning route home via Hazebrouck and the bars at Dunkerque, we found upon awakening on the Sunday morning *Shepperton Ferry* crossing that it was considerably more crowded than usual. It seemed, for whatever reason, that BEA (British European Airways) had cancelled some flights from Paris – the resultant crowds causing the E5011-hauled train to London to have a 30-minute late start.

12.01 Two of the numerous 2-8-2 141TC tanks at Paris Nord awaiting departure on Friday 8th November. Always at the country end of the train these push/pull services were sufficiently economic to await electrification of the system in 1970 rather than be replaced by diesels in the interim. 141TC34 was on the 0901 to Valmondais and by catching this train and hopping on and off the frequent services a further nine examples were caught that day – interrupted by the loss of my travel tickets (see text)!

93

CHAPTER THIRTEEN
NEARLY
THERE

13

THE CHAPTER HEADING OF COURSE REFERS TO my quest – burning ambition if you like – to obtain runs with 1,000 steam locomotives. The total now standing at 980, yet another visit to the Nord region (well, it was handy!) was undertaken. With the likelihood of the greater chance of 'new' haulages on the 141R-operated local services, I concentrated on them. Departing once more on the 'Night Ferry' from London, and as a result of a fog-delayed crossing, I eventually arrived at Dunkerque Ville on the Saturday morning, with a mere 15 minutes to wait for the 06:30 local to Hazebrouck – en route to Calais. It is impossible, looking back at my notes, to remember what the original plan was but I suspect it was varied, as the day went by, to suit where and when required locomotives turned up. Several short hops were made to, amongst other places, Etaples (where the steep cant of the track made alighting from a train somewhat precarious!) and Frethun – then an insignificant Calais suburb but now the location of the massive Chunnel freight yard. Similarly to earlier in the year in Britain, any steam (dead or alive) was noted – history was, after all, passing by. A commendable nine steam trains were caught which, taking into account the infrequency during certain times of the day, was very pleasing. Not so was the catch of 'new' engines – a mere three! Hazebrouck and the Dunkerque bars were visited once more en route home. Again, presumably delayed by the ever-present fog, the crossing with the only French-owned train ferry, the *Saint Germain*, arrived into Dover over an hour late – causing the E5014-operated London train to lose its path through Kent and arrive at 10:15 into Victoria. It was, however, an extremely pleasant Sunday morning journey through sleepy Kent, with the long train weaving its way via normally 100% electric-unit-operated routes through the Medway towns. It had that air of prestige about it and, with the 'wagon-lit' occupants yet to have their passport and custom checks, it is, now, a pleasant reminder of pre-terrorist days when security was not given the priority necessary in today's world. At Victoria, walking along past the 'wagon-lits' with the curtains/blinds now lifted, you could see an air of opulence – women with their fur stoles, men with clean crisp white shirts and their obligatory ties – the sight of which a lowly railway clerk could only envy. Who were these customers who could afford first-class sleeping berths for a through journey from Paris (11 hours rather than today's three!)? What were their jobs? How could they afford it? Would I one day aspire to such good fortune? I made my way home to the mundane suburb I had lived in all of my life, on a second-class 17-years-old bone-shaking cattle truck electric unit, with those thoughts still circulating in my mind. Writing this chapter 40 years later I suppose that if such a train still ran in today's world, it would be cluttered up with laptops, and passengers (or is it customers?) having to listen to the usually banal conversations mobile phone users resort to – in both first and second class accommodation!

1969 beckoned, and in the January the Beatles gave their last public performance – from the top of the Apple recording studios in London. March saw the first testing of Concorde at Toulouse and in July the event occurred that all those who were alive at the time can place themselves where they were when it happened – the landing of the first man on the moon. I personally was attempting, with some friends, to concentrate on a game of bar billiards, in a pub near Waterloo, which, with the television being positioned on the wall above the table, became impossible to complete! Oh and I nearly forgot that memorable Saturday in July at Hyde Park when the Rolling Stones held a free concert – then a novel idea. Although Brian Jones had died just two days previously it still went ahead, and perched halfway up a tree I could just about make out the group members on the stage – but at least I can claim I WAS THERE! Finally, in the August, British troops were deployed for the first time in Northern Ireland.

CHAPTER FOURTEEN

LAST RITES
OF THE *ARROW*

14

I HAD PLANNED TO DISCONTINUE TAKING EXHAUSTIVE NOTES of my travels, the original 'little red book' having been completely full with details of all journeys accomplished throughout 1968. On the horizon, however, was a six-country visit in the February of '69 so I purchased a second one which was unusual, bearing in mind adequate supplies at my workplace being usually 'available'. The second Saturday of January was to see the last steam hauled *La Fleche D'Or*. With no other planned variations, it was London to Paris on Friday's 'Night Ferry', returning on Saturday's *Golden Arrow* – in both instances, throughout their complete journeys. Never missing an opportunity to collect runs with the 141TCs, however, after arriving into Paris at 08:40 and with nearly four hours to fill before the last *Arrow*, the lure of collecting some more runs with the ever-present 141TCs was too great to ignore. After changing some money to buy a suburban timetable, a trip to Pontoise was made where, with 45 minutes to kill, I wandered around an enormous market which occupied eight streets – before heading back into Paris.

The 231K82-operated northbound *Arrow* has been well documented in various magazines – all I can add is I WAS ABOARD! With 231G81 on the preceding 08:10 semi and 231K22 on the southbound *Arrow*, it was the end of an era, all but just two of Calais' Pacifics surviving the following Monday's cull and being kept for ceremonial and rail tour duties. On the *Maid of Orleans* crossing back to 'Blighty' I gave some thought as to the future – without steam. It had been my main preoccupation over the last five years and, taking into consideration next month's bash, it was almost a certainty that my longed-for 1,000[th] steam locomotive would be caught. So what then?

Nothing had remotely interested me as much as the steam locomotive. Before that addiction had taken hold I had, with some school friends, often gone on walking or cycling weekends in Southern Britain, staying at youth hostels. I had lost touch with them – all my friends now being railway connected, some of whom, I am fortunate to say, having matured into lifelong relationships. I hardly knew any local persons of my own age in the area I lived because of the hundreds of days, and nights even, that I was away from home, travelling all over Britain and of course, latterly, Europe. Indeed my parents often stated that their home, to me, was just a B. & B! I would now have to integrate into a non-railway-peopled society. What had I got in common with them? That was perhaps the link because with my liking of the pub scene and need to get to know local people, these two aspects could be catered for by perhaps replying to an advert in the local paper for a bar person at my nearest pub. I cannot be sure, after all that time ago, whether this decision was acted upon before or after my February visit to Europe but, at least, by the end of that crossing some sort of life plan had been arrived at. Retrospectively, some of those 'new' local friends made when 'called to the bar' have also become lifelong friendships and nowadays, with little interest in today's railway scene, have become part and parcel of my life after steam.

PROPHETICALLY, ESPECIALLY IN VIEW OF MY THOUGHTS as detailed in the previous chapter, I wrote in my notebook upon leaving London on Thursday 20th February 1969 'one year after making my first continental bash we set forth for possibly my last'. This 11-day tour, starting from London on the 15:30 to Folkestone, amid the snow and slush left over from the previous night's blizzard, was indeed destined to be, apart from an occasional foray into Northern France, THE last big one. The demise of the steam locomotive throughout Europe was making it harder to find. Excessive electric and diesel mileage was being accumulated for just a few (in comparison) steam miles. This trip was started with a classic example – double-headed diesels from Calais to Amiens, the Nord Pacifics having been consigned to the history books last month.

Crossing Paris on the Metro system rather than using the through-vehicle portion of the Nord service – which took forever and a day via a circuitous route around the suburbs – we arrived before it, thus giving us a greater choice of seats on the overnight train departing from the impressive Lyon station at 23:46. The eight-hour journey – exchanging overhead electric for a third rail cousin at Chambery, via the Frejus tunnel (at 8½ miles, merely the 25th longest in the world) – found us, on the Friday morning, at the border crossing town of Modane. The weather had turned from a relatively mild Paris to a decidedly nippy Italy. Coming down from the Alps into Torino on the *Il Piemonte*, a Lyon Perrache to Torino multiple unit express, the reason became clear. Heavy fresh falls of snow had coated the countryside which, being bathed by glorious sunshine, set the scene for two Englishmen off on a skiing holiday – or so fellow travellers might have assumed. Little did they know! Changing at Torino into another multiple unit we finally arrived for, hopefully, our first Italian steam, at Cavallermaggiore – 22 hours after starting our quest.

The same premise as last year's visit i.e. selecting non-railcar-indicated services in the public timetable, again worked and the 13:51 departure to Alessandria was in the hands of 880.038. In true Italian tradition, a mere eight miles into our journey, at Bra, we exchanged locomotives – with 640.121 taking over for the remaining 52¾ miles. For 3½ hours this train made its leisurely way across snow-covered plains, enhanced by brilliant sunshine, of Northern Italy. Starting with two coaches and one van and collecting a further seven vans at Alba, I would have loved to have been positioned somewhere in the adjacent fields taking photographs of it. Every half hour or so we interconnected with various railcar- or electric locomotive-hauled trains at junction stations – also passing two Crosti-boilered 743s on freights en route. All good things come to an end and a tight connection into a Vercelli line railcar enabled us to get as far up the line as Casale Monferrato after which, with a couple of changes, runs with two further 640s were collected. The first 640 was on a packed commuter train from the university city of Vercelli but the second was unexpectedly crowded with under 25s. Noisy but no trouble, they all alighted at the decidedly unremarkable hamlet of Lemelle – was it a rave – we will never know. We had, unwittingly, uncovered the first of two Alessandria-allocated locomotive diagrams – the Pavia service, being worked by the same 640 as had brought us in from Bra. Having covered the route into Pavia, we wanted to return the 40 miles back to Alessandria for the next day's steam services but the last train had long gone – even at 21:00 hours! So, to kill time and to obtain free accommodation overnight, we travelled via Milano and Torino, arriving at Alessandria at 03:44 on the Saturday morning – 175 miles instead of 40! The 02:37 from Torino must have been Italy's answer to our TPOs, it being formed of two passenger coaches in the middle of 20 vans!

Although a considerable amount of snow was left from a blizzard two days previously, the air, even at that time of the morning, was very mild and it was not at all cold overnight. Two new routes for steam haulage were then covered on the 03:58 Alessandria to Vercelli and the 05:52 from there to Pavia. Unfortunately, from a haulage point of view, uncovering the second locomotive diagram with 640,019 working both trains. En route, at Casale, we witnessed, but annoyingly were unable to catch 685.008 on a connecting service. A short hop up to Milano – and the three hours there gave us plenty of time to view Italy's second largest city. Indeed, it now has its own Metro system, thus emphasising the sheer volume of people requiring transportation. We decided against viewing any of the catwalk/fashion shows Milano is famous for as we had already had the unshaven faces and the bedraggled look travel-stained enthusiasts always succumbed to, and would probably have been refused entry anyway. The weather had now turned to heavy rain, which did not help our appearance, as we walked to the Porto Garibaldi suburban terminus. From this surprisingly modern station, an ancient (in comparison) Class 625 steam locomotive was in charge of the 14:38 departure to Cremona. There were two aspects of this journey which made it special. Firstly, compared with our previous visit to Cremona last year, there was a considerable increase in the number of diesel locomotives in circulation so we considered ourselves fortunate that it was steam at all. Secondly, the first 21 miles of this journey, to the junction station of the Cremona branch at Treviglio, was on the electrified main line across Northern Italy from Torino to Venezia and was thoroughly savoured as being the longest 'steam under the wires' train we had been on. Alighting at Treviglio, planning to cover the route onwards to Cremona the next day, we travelled a further 30 miles along the main line to Brescia for the only southbound steam loco-operated train of the day along that route to Cremona – the 18:22 departure. Between then and mid-morning the following day we dodged from line to line in the area in an (eventually successful) attempt to cover all lines radiating from Cremona with steam traction. 625.149 was on the 18:22 departure, taking us to the junction station of Olmeneta, where we changed onto a Treviglio line service – falling foul of diesel haulage. Things were changing in the area because the 20:38 departure for Mantova (last year's luxury 685-operated service) was also a diesel. Conceding defeat in steam-searching for the night, we booked in at a local hotel at the princely sum of 1200 lira (£4.80) – but managed to pop out to Cava Tigozzi, the first station on the Codogno branch, to get a 2½-mile run with another representative of the Class 880, before hitting the sack.

One of Cremona's claims to fame lies with its football team who, in 1993, beat Derby County at Wembley to win the Anglo-Italian Cup – apparently only the second ever Italian team to do that. This meant everything to a nation that is madly passionate about its football – but nothing to a steam crank like me! Sunday morning dawned, shrouded in fog and, much to the proprietor's amazement; we left before breakfast, catching the 07:05 to Treviglio – the final steam route from Cremona that required our attention. Alighting there, and having congratulated ourselves on achieving the somewhat problematic accomplishment of covering ALL available lines with steam haulage, we progressed to the next area – Brescia. This city was devastated in 1769 when lightning struck a church, igniting a nearby gunpowder storage depot, causing a massive explosion destroying a large part of the city and killing 3,000 people. Our target on this final day in Italy was the route from this rebuilt city to Lecco. The 11:15 departure had 625.215 in charge and, because of our self-imposed restriction to travel only on steam loco-operated services, we were unable to make the lakeside destination of Lecco itself, at the southern end of Lake Como, returning from the junction station of Calolziocorte Olginate a few miles short. Nevertheless, over five hours of glorious mountainside scenery, causing the locomotives to be heard for a change, were enjoyed over our first gradient-strewn journey with Italian steam. Chronic overcrowding of main line services was, and still is, endemic throughout Italy and our two-hour jaunt onwards to Venezia was no exception. Upon arrival there, chicken and chips were hungrily devoured in readiness for our international train to the next country.

Italian steam suffered a slow lingering death and, by the mid 70s, was to be found acting mainly as standbys or on localised shunting duties. However I am somewhat amazed that all the secondary lines travelled on in my visits during 1968/9 in Italy are still in operation at the time of writing (2009) – albeit obviously now devoid of steam – but with slightly improved services and frequencies often being the case. Had these routes been located in Britain, there would have been no way they would have survived. The FS (Ferrovie Dello Stato – Italian State railways) system being a subsidised, nationalised industry is the probable explanation, and railways providing a transport service to/for the public obviously achieves higher priority there than in the privatised British version.

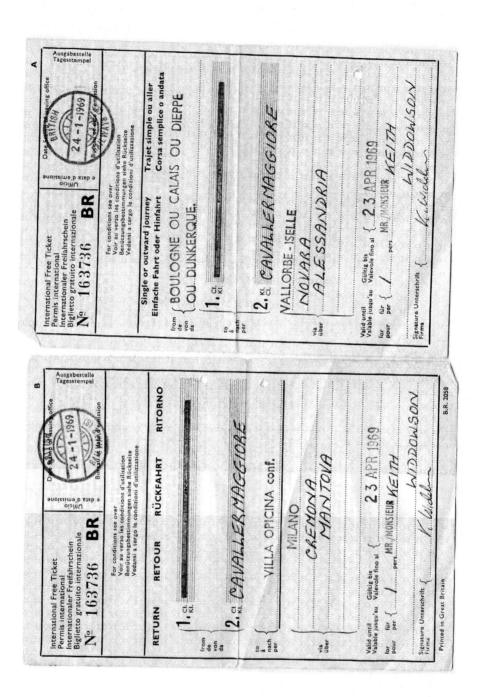

15.01   2-6-0 640.121 waits time at Alba with the 1351 Cavallermaggiore to Alessandria on Friday 21st February 1969. It was here that a further seven vans were added before the leisurely 60 mile 3½ hour journey across the plains of Northern Italy was continued.

CHAPTER SIXTEEN
AN ARRESTING EXPERIENCE
16

EPARTING VENEZIA SAINT LUCIA THAT SUNDAY NIGHT, it was with a certain amount of apprehension that our journey into the communist-held country of Yugoslavia was embarked upon. General Tito had held this disparate mix of ethnic differences together for many years but, as its turbulent history has well documented, his grip was weakening and, after his death, the resulting combination of western influences and cultural differences ripped Yugoslavia to shreds. Indeed, there had been serious student riots in the capital of Beograd only the previous year! The eight-hour overnight train via Trieste and Sezana to Zidani, a wayside halt by Western standards, can be best described by quoting from my notes made at the time – 'not the best of overnights with a big wedge as far as Trieste followed by continual interruption by customs and passport officials of both countries – sleeping for a mere three hours!'

A certain amount of information as to the possibility of steam-hauled passenger services had filtered through the crank network and, sure enough, after just over an hour's wait we were heading south on the main line to Zagreb behind 06.218 – one of the 2-8-2s seen the previous year at the Austrian border station of Spielfeld Strab. Two hours and 53 miles later (as our trip progressed, it became obvious that timekeeping was not a priority throughout Yugoslavia), and having travelled through some quite spectacular mountainous terrain, we arrived at what was to become the provincial capital of Croatia – Zagreb. The route had all the infrastructure work in connection with electrification in situ but was not yet operative – American-designed General Motors diesels working the International services and steam powering the secondary stoppers. Our next destination was the then capital city of Yugoslavia – Beograd, some 250 miles distant. There were insufficient – or perhaps even no – local trains across the northern section of this central, somewhat barren part of the country so we had to endure a diesel-operated journey aboard the *Jugoslavija Express*. Originally planning to join a local train from Vrpolje (a town to the south of 'the great plains') at its starting point, because of the late running of the International train we had to stay on board looking out at all calling points until we eventually overtook it on the single-tracked main line at Sid – where we gratefully alighted from the, by then, 45 minutes late-running International service. The 51-mile journey (still on the main line) was plagued by delays both through being looped for other trains to pass and the locomotive (11.059) taking water – eventually arriving at the junction station (with the line to Subotica) of Stara Pazova over an hour late. The reason for not continuing through to the capital was the aforementioned quest to travel behind as many different steam locomotives as possible, and taking into consideration that our train south from Beograd was not until 23:00 that evening, we had some time in hand to 'check them out'. Our plans to travel up the branch, perhaps to the first town, were scuppered as a result of all the delays previously encountered. Stara Pazova, a mere 22 miles north of Beograd, was not, and perhaps still isn't, a tourist's destination, and by opting to spend some time there waiting for a steam service off the branch, we became objects of curiosity amongst the station refreshment room customers. We were unable to see exactly what motive power each incoming train had on the front so every time an arrival was imminent, off we trooped to the platform, witnessed the inevitable diesel, and returned for another coffee. I failed to note how many occasions this scenario was repeated but it was enough to arouse the suspicions of the ever-present communist guards. Two machine-gun-equipped representatives menacingly 'escorted' us to a small room somewhere at the back of the station, equipped with one table and two chairs and illuminated with a single light bulb dangling from the ceiling. This 'interrogation' room was more akin to a prison cell, and having taken our passports (perhaps the most worrying aspect of the entire proceeding), they wanted to know what we were doing and why were we there. At least, I assume they were asking that. Emptying our cases and rucksacks, exposing our films etc. and speaking no English, they were unmoved when presented with a British railway magazine showing pictures of steam trains – with us pointing to them saying that was what we were doing and that it was an 'acceptable' hobby in the UK. Eventually a 'signal controller' who spoke German was brought into the room. Bill and I had an appreciation of the language and, more importantly, a phrase book – which became the essential tool for communication. After what seemed hours but presumably was a lot shorter, our mediator explained to us that he had convinced the guards that we were not spying and that, as fellow railway employees from England, we presented no security risk. We were still kept in the room until the last train of the day to Beograd had arrived then, with our passports begrudgingly returned to us, we were escorted to the train and 'seen away' – being advised to stay on International services in future. Were we arrested? I don't know. Many years later a visiting group of UK plane spotters was arrested and thrown into jail – released only after bail was paid by their parents back in the UK. At their trial, the authorities stated that aircraft were classified as military equipment and, as such, they were spying. Only after political intervention affirming, as if paraphrasing our pleas, that such activities are hobbies in Britain, were they exonerated. Retrospectively, we were fortunate that a similar fate could have awaited us if it hadn't been for the intervention of a fellow railway employee. It was a few minutes into the journey, too shaken by all the events, that we both realised that the noise from the front was – yes, a steam engine. That cheered us up, and upon arriving at Beograd, the only station in Yugoslavia which had concrete platforms, we discovered it was an 01 (2-6-2) – yet another new class for us.

Summing up our first day's travel I think that, compared to other European countries bashed, Yugoslavia was a dangerous, oppressive country with an overall impression of poverty. Scenes at the small wayside stopping points (stations would be too grand a description) saw numerous families, with what seemed to be their lifetime's possessions with them, dressed in worn ragged clothing, attempting to escape from their dreary surroundings – not helped by the poor, rain-swept, muddy conditions prevailing throughout our visit. We became the point of interest for many fellow travellers - but luckily, not for the on-board commie guards – with attempted conversation and the occasional begging requests. The one 'plus' factor of our adventure were the steam engines themselves which were always externally clean and seemingly up to the task. We, by ignoring the guards' 'recommendations', continued to catch them on local trains and were rewarded with mile after mile of steam haulage – long since disappeared from the British scene and increasingly so throughout Europe.

Tuesday night's accommodation was to be the 23:00 Beograd to Skopje. This was a city which was almost destroyed six years previously when a major earthquake killed over 1,000 people and made 120,000 more homeless with the ruins of the railway station remaining today as a memorial to the victims – part of a specially created museum. The plan was to get as far along the main line to Greece as possible – before retracing our steps to Zagreb en route to Austria. It was all new track of course – I was not to know then that the following year, returning from a 'civilian' holiday, I was to cover the entire route (albeit with diesel) whilst travelling from the Greek Islands via Munich en route home. Departing behind a Class 05 Pacific, piloted for the first 68 miles to Lapovo by a Class 38 (2-8-0), was sheer heaven, falling into a surprisingly deep sleep listening to the sound of double-headed steam. In the early hours, at Nis, a second Pacific took over and, having been delayed through the night by the sheer volume of people (particularly south of Nis) and the apparent willingness to loop the train at every opportunity, we baled out at 10:25 in the morning. The train was, by then, running 78 minutes late, which was as far as we dared go without jeopardising plans for the remainder of the week. An eight-minute connection into the 06:32 Skopje to Belgrade opposite way working turned into, unsurprisingly, a 37-minute one! This was the one – my 1,000[th] steam locomotive for haulage. I had finally achieved the, to me, magic figure. Again changing Pacifics at their allocated depot, Nis, another 200 miles of steam were enjoyed. After a 56 minutes late arrival into the capital, the first (and only) meal in Yugoslavia was devoured in the form of a 'potato/pork salad' – my memory failing as to exactly what else it comprised.

Wednesday night's accommodation was the 23:40 *Slovenija Express* Beograd to Zagreb. Having been fooled by a lack of ticket checks on the last two trains, we opted for first-class again – this time, however, being excessed to the tune of 17 dinars 80-something for the privilege. It was crowded, and we were so tired it was worth it and, for once, late running was to our benefit – causing reduced waiting time for our connection forward at Zagreb. A wonderful daylight five hours of steam haulage on the 08:00 departure to Maribor was then relished – more so because *one* of the vehicles on the train actually had an operative water system. A full wash, shave etc. made us feel – as well as probably look – better! At Maribor, where a collection of ancient Austrian steam locomotives was noted, another 06 took us over the border to Austria. A summary of our Yugoslavian steam travels was seven trains, 11 locos from five classes for 667½ miles.

16.01 This Yugoslavian 2-8-2 06.006, having previously brought us tender first across the border within the previous hour, is seen returning to Maribor with the 1548 from the Austrian border station of Spielfeld Strass on Wednesday 26th February 1969. We were now relaxing after two very uneasy days spent in communist Yugoslavia where, as foreigners off the beaten track (and 'arrested' to boot), we felt every move was being monitored.

16.02   The first train in two days travelling through Yugoslavia that had running water and
therefore allowed us the ability to clean/wash/shave! Wednesday 26th February 1969 and
2-8-2 06.021 arrives at Zagreb with the stock for our 0800 to Maribor departure.

I HAVE TO SAY – BASED ON OUR experiences over the previous few days – that upon arriving at Spielfeld Strab on the Wednesday afternoon, a sense of relief was felt at having escaped the tension and feeling of oppression seemingly surrounding us over the last few days. No **more furtive** note-taking or the feeling of being watched. A year had passed **since we had** vowed to return here – behind steam locomotives we had witne**ssed during** the early hours of that freezing morning. With that mission **accomplished we could** now concentrate on visiting some more lines in Austria – hopefully still steam-worked – that we had missed or were unable to encompass within the time limitations last year. Our visit to Spielfeld this year was at a far more reasonable hour, 15:30, just right for the afternoon 'peak' of services – still fortunately steam-operated – between there and Graz. The 'peak' was, in reality, a mere three more passenger trains that day, northbound to Graz, the route being primarily freight orientated – the first being the grandly named *Ljubljana Express*. This arrived, similar to our border crossing service 1½ hours previously, hauled by a Yugoslavian Class 06 – with just two coaches. It seemed that all trains, whether long or short distance services, were reduced to two vehicles whilst crossing the border – presumably to make the customs/ passport checks easier. The Yugoslavian locomotive was exchanged for an Austrian one and 52.7070, together with two further coaches, departed at 16:40. The first stop on this train was at Leibnitz where we alighted for the following stopper, 11 minutes later, with another 52 taking us the 22 miles on to Graz. Although, annoyingly, having to catch 52.7070 again back down the line to Werndorf, it was worth it because the last train of the day, the 17.

28 from Radkersburg (a 20-mile-long branch-line from Spielfeld boasting a meagre three trains per day!), was yet another new Class 52.

So there we were, at Graz at 20:00, with no planned steam travel until 12 hours hence – and that was from Wien, a mere 135 miles distant. After suitable sustenance courtesy of the station buffet, a study of the timetable, to find the slowest possible journey to the capital, revealed a loop line from Wiener Neustadt to Wien via Wampersdorf. Not only did it serve the purpose of killing time overnight but there were two departures, at 04:32 and 04:56, which did not have a railcar depicted at the top of the column – thus indicating 'loco-operated'. Departing Graz on the 22:14, we then 'festered' at Bruck for two hours before catching the three-coach ten-vanfit 01:25 train towards Wien in the early hours of Thursday morning. With long station dwell times, for parcels/papers etc, we somehow stayed awake in order to alight at Wiener Neustadt at four a.m. by taking it in turns to keep our sleep-laden eyes open by nudging/kicking each other when the occasion demanded it – would it all be worth it, we wondered? Well, the first train had a 52 on it and the second a 77 – wonderful 'catches' and well worth the inconvenience of alighting from the warm main line train on that cold dark morning. Most European commuter services run irrationally early in the morning and Austria was the earliest of the lot! Both trains were unbelievably packed but the commuters kindly gave us 'smelly English dossers' a wide berth!

Arriving at Wien Sudbahnhof at 06:30, we had just over 1½ hours to locate the 'country' departure terminus of Stammersdorf. Our plans, however, were thrown into disarray because of a breakdown of some description on the Metro system – causing us to take a four-mile hair-raising taxi ride at 71 schillings (£4.50). I say 'country' because it was the furthest terminus from the city centre and, upon arrival, it was just a couple of unkempt platforms squeezed between some nondescript buildings. Luckily, the taxi driver knew where he was going, having been shown the railway timetable with us pointing to the Stammersdorf entry. Looking at the current city maps, Stammersdorf appears to have been relegated to a tram stop – presumably the OBB station having long since closed. Class 93.1333 worked the 07:58 departure to Huhenau which, for the 2¾ hour 56-mile journey, enabled some sleep to be recovered. The daily farce at Grob Schweinbarth (see chapter three) still continued in its usual unhurried/unproductive way. You would have thought that, having visited this 'model railway' system previously, nothing more could surprise us. Well, we were wrong because at Dobermannsdorf, a mere five miles short of our destination of Huhenau, a railcar propelled a van onto the rear of the train and stayed attached. Upon arrival at Hohenau, they were promptly detached to form a returning service to Wien Praterstern! The purpose of our return to the Mistelbach 'system' was an attempt to complete coverage of all the myriad of routes. Some lines, however, escaped us – mainly because we just could not cater for their inclusion in our allotted timespan. As an example, one line – from Laa an der Thaya to Sigmundsherberg – had no departures between 04:25 and 12:02! Later that day, after a liquid lunch at Mistelbach, it was noted in the timetable that the particular service we planned to travel on stood at Grob Schweinbarth for 36 minutes before continuing its journey forward. This enabled us to return to Pirawarth, three miles back, whence we came, and catch what turned out to be a double-headed service, changing back onto our original train which was still waiting at the junction station. You couldn't make it up! At Ganserndorf we caught an electric train for the 16 miles to Floridsdorf in the hope that the 16:57 Praterstern to Bernhardstal was steam-worked. This was a one-minute connection – between trains in opposite directions! Taking into consideration that the Praterstern train ran over the electrified main line for the majority of its journey to within three miles of the Czechoslovakian border town of Breclav, we were elated (to say the least) when 77.11 appeared for the 43 ½-mile run – only just squeezing onto the packed train. Returning to Wien on more mundane transport, a frankfurter and bread 'meal' was devoured before travelling, for the first time, out of Wien's modern Westbahnhof station on the 23:10 *Wien-Holland Express*.

Another 'let's kill the time' overnight variation en route to our eventual destination was then enacted. Had we alighted at our required destination of Amstetten off the express on that Friday morning, it would have meant a 5½-hour fester. So we went through to Wels (01:47 – 02:54), returning to Amstetten (close to the notorious Mauthausen concentration camp) at the more acceptable hour of 04:15. Why do all this, the reader might wonder – travelling/changing at very unsocial times overnight. I can only repeat the previous explanation given during the previous year's bash. It was necessary in order to avoid overnight accommodation costs and to catch early morning steam services otherwise missed out on.

The line from Amstetten to Klein Reifling had, since our last visit, been electrified but it seemed OBB had yet to resource sufficient ELs for the services – the beneficial results (from our point of view) being a return trip over the 28-mile delightfully scenic route with two different 78s – and the first journey being particularly splendid with dawn breaking over snow-capped mountains. Although the reason for our many journeys throughout Europe was essentially steam-chasing, the benefit was visiting parts, in this case certainly, of the country off the beaten tourist trails with the resultant wonderful panoramic scenery being thoroughly enjoyed and never forgotten. After that, a short hop to Austria's third largest city, Linz, where, having heard through the grapevine that some rush hour services were still steam-operated, we enjoyed an early afternoon cooked meal at the OBB canteen at the depot. Having bashed the depot and seen some Class 50s (of German descent with different smoke deflectors), 52s and 93s, the 'director' told us no Dampfloks worked out of Linz on passenger services. I can only assume that the language translation somehow lost its way because the 17:05 departure to the border (with Czechoslovakia) town of Summerau had 52.7017 as large as life waiting to work it. The sparse service did not allow us to go all the way so we baled out at Gaisbach-Wartberg (16¾ miles) and caught an OBB bus of Bedford pre-war vintage to Mauthausen (the line having closed some years previously) where a connecting diesel locomotive-operated service took us back to the main line at St Valentin. An abortive wait to view two Klein Reifling services on the off-chance they were steam preceded a return to Linz for the 22:25 International train to Zurich en route home – via steam in both West Germany and France, of course.

In Austria, by 1974, only 250 steam locomotives remained – Class 52s being in the majority. Vienna North shed closed in December of that year – four rush hour workings out of the Praterstern station remaining, Class 77-operated until then. The Iron Ore Railway at Vordernberg (Class 97) and the Lower Austria services centred at Mistelbach (Class 93), however, still saw some steam operated passenger services. The Summerau route from Linz, in the process of electrification, also had isolated steam workings. I am just appreciative of the fact that I witnessed Austrian steam when I did – forever etched in my memory bank.

ARRIVING AT ZURICH ON THE SATURDAY MORNING, we had two hours to kill so, unlike in a lot of cities visited throughout my European trips, we actually ventured outside and did some shopping – in my case, buying a Rolling Stones LP at well below British prices! Heading north, a new border crossing (to me) was utilised to get into West Germany – that between Koblenz and Waldshut. This one-car electric unit took a mere five minutes to cross the River Rhine – customs and passports being dealt with upon arrival. I remember how proud I was always, showing the solid blue passport, in a purpose-made leather case of course, at all the custom checks throughout Europe – looking at the pitiful small ones held by most other travellers. Now we all have those inferior ones – how times have changed! On shed at Waldshut was 50.2838 and, upon enquiring, we were told she was to work our 13:16 departure to Basle – she was the same locomotive on the same train we had seen last September and had promised ourselves to return for – because of its uniqueness of steam into the Swiss city of Basle. It was one of two isolated passenger trains within a Radolfzell freight duty which returned the following day on an 08:22 opposite-way working. Upon arrival at the DB station at Basle, we went through the customs etc, and caught a tram across to the main SBB station (Schweizerische Bundesbahn – Swiss Federal Railways), going through customs again to gain access to the French part of the station, all in 28 minutes! A short trip took us to Mulhouse, visited several times exactly a year ago, to find no steam activity – at least, not during our time there. We had heard through the grapevine that a once-a-day steam train ran from Strasbourg to Saarbrucken and, with nothing to lose, headed for it. With what seemed like an exceptional amount of diesel and electric locomotives in circulation, the welcome sight of a solitary 141R backing down onto the 18:41 departure made our deviation all the more worth while. 141R375 took us on a delightful 71-mile journey across the border to Saarbrucken – all the more appreciated because all other services passing, be they freight or passenger, were not steam. Three further West German steam locomotives were caught in a mini blitz on Saarbrucken's suburban services during which we noted the somewhat unique push/pull trains using Class 23s which of course were tender locomotives.

This was our seventh night without having slept between clean sheets, and sheer tiredness caused me to fall asleep in a café – face first into a bowl of soup! Whether we were made to leave, presumably looking like vagrants with several days' growth on our faces, I fail to remember but we managed to catch the 01:36 on that Sunday morning to Metz. Boy, were we glad to see the 21:50 Milano Centrale to Calais train turn up. It meant six hours homeward bound without having to worry about changing trains or oversleeping. The ever reliable provision of one of Boulogne's 141Rs took us the final few miles across the snowy plains of Northern France connecting into the Folkestone bound *Saint Patrick*. For the last four days, since leaving Yugoslavia, all our trains had never been more than a few minutes late but British Rail's timekeeping was par for the course. The 14:27 to Victoria suffered a 27-minute delay in attempting to climb the bank from Folkestone Harbour to the main line – albeit in sleety conditions.

18.01 West German steam into Swiss city of Basle – it had to be done. This one isolated working
had been noted some six months earlier and we went well out of our way, when returning
home from Austria, to catch it. 2-10-0 50.2838 was exactly the same locomotive as seen
previously on exactly the same train – the remainder of her duty being on local freight
workings. She is seen here at the intermediate station of Dogern whilst working the 1316
Walshut to Basle on Saturday 1st March 1969.

CHAPTER NINETEEN

MAD AS A MARCH HARE

19

THE LITTLE RED NOTEBOOK, DELIBERATELY PURCHASED FOR 1969's exploits with steam trains had by now, a mere three months into that year, fallen into disuse because, for this March trip, there was not a lot recorded other than the actual steam runs themselves on the back of scrap paper! It was the last Friday in March and an unproblematic on-time journey on the 'Night Ferry' saw us arrive at Paris at 08:40. Starting again with the 09:10 departure we (Dave and I) visited what is now a list of long-forgotten, and mostly unpronounceable, suburban destinations. Here's a couple – Champ de Courses d'Enghien and La Barre-Ormesson. Five hours later, by switching trains often involving making same-minute cross-platform connections – probably, to the onlooker, acting 'as mad as a March Hare' – we had achieved runs with 13 different examples of these competent efficient tanks.

Back to the main line and, avoiding the now dieselised fasts, the 14:27 semi was taken forward from Amiens by the expected 141R, noting en route, at Abbeville, 141R116 presumably deputising for a railcar failure, on a connecting Le Treport service. I was fortunate enough, at this late stage, to obtain four required Boulogne-allocated 141Rs that day. A minor variation to previous homeward bound trips from the Northern port bashes was that, instead of 'going out on the town' at Dunkerque, we instead spent nearly three hours at Lille – before catching the 'Night Ferry' home – perhaps having exhausted all of Dunkerque's drinking establishments. A reportedly smooth crossing courtesy of the *Twickenham Ferry* doesn't explain why the London train had a 36-minute late start from Dover Marine that Sunday morning – but then neither can I!

CHAPTER TWENTY

THAT'S ALL, FOLKS

20

I N September of 1969 I have listed in my 'runs book' four journeys with 141Rs – all in the Calais area. Having traced back within other non-steam documentation, I can see that I had come over on the 'Night Ferry' but had not bashed the Nord suburban steam services prior to catching the Calais train – which was 141R-hauled from Amiens. I can honestly say that as I am writing this, it came to me that Dave and I had gone 'tourist' – by visiting, amongst other sights, the Eiffel Tower. From 1970, all further runs with 141Rs were pure luck, being caught either on the way to or from holiday destinations in the south of France, Berlin, Yugoslavia or the Greek islands. Having done some research on Boulogne's allocation of 141Rs during the 1968/9 period, I think that I only, in the end, missed four of the home depot's stud of these elephant-eared survivors – all of whom, sadly, were sent to the cutter's torch in May 1971. Summing up the French scene, by the time of my travels there were only 800 steam locomotives in SNCF stock. Paris suburbs went in Dec '70, Nord in May '71, Ouest in Sep '71 – leaving isolated and unpredictable instances (mainly 141Rs) being reported elsewhere. Some would say that Sarreguemines, whilst still being visited by DB steam, perhaps became the final throw of the dice – with 141R73 working freights as late as March 1974. Others would quote the CFTA system (Chemin de Fer Touristique du Vermandois), leased from SNCF, as witness to the final French steam – with 140Cs surviving there into 1975. Similarly to Britain, however, there are nowadays many excursions using preserved steam on the main lines – but it's not the same knowing that your train will be steam worked rather than hoping that it might be!

I was transported back in time to this happy part of my life when compiling this book and often, when reading out aloud to my ever patient wife some of the jottings from my two little red books, she nods sympathetically, wondering, perhaps, what a different world I had inhabited prior to meeting her. I don't regret a thing although, with hindsight and perhaps the experience which age brings, if I had started 'chasing' as soon as I'd joined the railways then perhaps I might have made a possible 2,000th! I sincerely hope the reader has enjoyed following my European exploits as much as I have writing them.

WHILST READING THROUGH SOME OLD *RAILWAY WORLD* magazines, I chanced upon an article by M. T. Hedderly in the September 1970 edition dealing with the demise of French express passenger steam locomotives during the 1968-69 season. As part of the story he was privileged to have ridden on the footplate of the above train – ON WHICH I WAS A PASSENGER! The following is an extract from that article:

Having learnt that the end of express passenger steam was imminent, I decided to visit France over the Autumn Bank Holiday in 1968. My main objective was the Bourbonnais route and the SNCF kindly supplied me with a footplate pass for the crack Train 1109 rapide.

The Bourbonnais line leaves the electrified PLM main line at Moret-les-Sablons, 41½ miles from Paris, and strikes due south to Clermont Ferrand, 260½ miles from the capital, by way of the Upper Loire Valley, then its tributary the Allier to the famous spa of Vichy. The ruling gradients are 1 in 167 between Moret and Nevers (except for the two miles at 1 in 125 either side of La Charite) and 1 in 200 between Nevers and St Germain-des-Fosses, where the St Etienne and Lyon line diverges. The section from St Germain to Clermont includes the gruelling six-mile climb at 1 in 91 to Randan tunnel.

With its booking of 269 minutes for the 219 miles from Moret to Clermont, inclusive of eight intermediate stops totalling 19 minutes,

Train 1109 long constituted the most arduous assignment remaining for steam traction in France. The load was regularly 600 tons as far as Nevers where engines were changed and three coaches were detached. On Fridays, however, the full load was always taken through to Clermont, so I deliberately chose to make my footplate journey on a Friday in order to see how the 4-8-2 coped with the 600-ton load throughout. The Friday schedule was identical as far as Vichy but an extra three minutes were allowed over Randan to Riom, and a further minute between Riom and Clermont.

It was drizzling as I made my way into the depot besides Moret station on August 30th. This small depot has no allocation of its own but is used as a stabling point for diesel and steam power off the Bourbonnais line, and for electric locomotives that work the Bourbonnais trains to and from the capital. After making my presence and purpose known to the sous-chef, I was introduced to the Nevers crew with whom I was to ride. It only remained for me to don my bleus in the sous-chef's office, typical of its kind with its floor covering of highly polished linoleum and two pairs of footpads strategically placed beside the desk!

241P24 was to be the engine as far as Nevers and after stowing my hand luggage in the tender, I clambered up into the cab, which would be quite roomy were it not for the plated casing of the mechanical stoker standing nearly a foot off the floor and about 18 inches wide, bisecting the footplate. It makes a convenient perch while the crew busy themselves with last minute preparations. It was good to experience anew the unique atmosphere of the footplate – the hiss and sing of steam, wispy air, faces tinged with flickering firelight; and, in place of the clang of the shovel, the churning of the stoker screw. The array of gauges is impressive to British eyes and includes refinements like high and low pressure steam chest pressure dials. Grouped conveniently in front of the fireman's seat on the right-hand side are the stoker controls.

The fire was inspected before we left; it was surprisingly thin and almost completely flat on the wide bed of the firebox, for all the small lumps of coal squirted in by the steam jets of the stoker undergo combustion before they reach the firebox floor. The temperature in the cab was noticeably cooler than on manually fired engines as the firebox door, above the stoker, is normally opened only to inspect the fire. Soon we were moving softly off shed up to Postetwo, then backing down to the station to wait in the bay for our train to arrive.

Traffic was heavy that day; the Nevers crew could not remember ever having seen so many of their colleagues at Moret before – there being eight sets of Nevers men there simultaneously, off freights with 141Rs. Passenger traffic was heavy too, for in addition to the Fridays-only 19:00 Paris–Nevers relief there was a further Bourbonnais train behind, which was to go forward with a 141R. The diesel for the 19:00 came off shed to join us in the station as dusk fell.

Soon Train 1109 rolled in and the electric locomotive came off, slightly behind time. As we coupled up to the train, the chef de train handed the driver the 'bulletin de composition' which gave the load as 13 vehicles, 606 tonnes – the load limit for the timing being 650 tonnes as far as St Germain. Taking into consideration one vehicle was a bogie van and that, being a Friday, the second class vehicles were full and standing, I assessed the load to be 545 tons tare and 605 tons gross.

Departure from Moret was two minutes late, but an energetic start was made and we passed kilometre post 69, 1.40 miles out and top of the ¾ mile at 1 in 167, in three minutes 31seconds at 39mph. Cut-off was reduced to 50/55 per cent at this point and to 40/45 per cent on the succeeding undulations skirting the southern edge of the Foret de Fontainbleau, which enabled the 1¾ mile rise at 1 in 167 to the summit just beyond Montigny to be climbed with a fall in speed only from 62 to 60 mph. The Flaman speed recorder on the 241Ps is placed on the fireman's side, facing the driver across the cab, and I was able to read it and the pressure gauges quite easily by the electric light from my position standing behind the driver. I checked the Flaman against my stopwatch and found it accurate. I regret that I was not able to observe the changes of cut-off as closely as I should have liked, not wishing to disturb Driver Brillaux too much, but 40/45 per cent hp/lp was the general position once we were into speed, with changes being made on the regulator.

The stops at the principal stations on the Bourbonnais line tend to be approached extremely slowly, sometimes because of speed restrictions and elsewhere because the letter of the law is adhered to on SNCF's peculiar rule that stops should be approached at walking pace. Montargis is the worst; the only trains which do not call there are the two first class only autorails which are authorised to pass through 'en marche àvue' at a maximum of 30 kph providing the driver has observed an all-right hand-signal from the station inspector!

Between Montargis and Gien, the line climbs out of the Loing valley over to the Loire; there is a gradual rise over the 11.75 miles from Solterres to a summit at Pk148, with a total of six miles at between 1 in 167 and 182. Speeds of 64-5mph were maintained on all the 1 in 167 sections with 40/45 per cent hp/lp cut-offs used throughout. Time keeping demands this standard of performance.

No 241P24 averaged 71.8mph from Briare to Myennes and despite steam being shut off at two points (before both Bonny-sur-Loire and Neuvy) with speed allowed to drift down to 70mph, the Gien-Cosne section was run in even time precisely, start-to-stop. A traction inspector, in charge of two trainees returning to Nevers, had boarded the engine at Gien and I had reason to be thankful for his presence on this stage, for the wind caught my beret as I leaned out trying to spot kilometre posts in the dark. I thought I had seen the last of my Gallic headgear (some form of head covering is essential on steam in France in view of the gritty coal) but amazingly the inspector had caught it in flight.

We were two minutes late on leaving Cosne because of station overtime here and at two other places. This was easily recouped on the 40 minutes booking thence to Nevers, which presumably contains a margin of recovery time.

An extremely cautious approach was made round the curves to Nevers, with a slight signal check outside. Nevertheless, the arrival was a minute early and I was able to congratulate Driver Brillaux on a fine run before hurrying down from the engine to retrieve my luggage from the locker at the rear of the tender while 241P24 was uncoupled. Six minutes are allowed for engine changing. The engine, which was to take Train 1109 forward, was 241P8, not in as good external condition as her sister; the crew was again from Nevers.

Departure was ½ minute late, but we had barely attained 40 mph when the driver partially closed the regulator while the fireman struggled to get the train heating working. The effort was successful and away we blazed again, until the regulator was closed to bring speed within the 56 mph limit over the junction north of Saincaize. The great engine was opened up through the station to sustain 62mph on the succeeding 1 in 250 rise and 71½ in the dip beyond. At this point, the driver evidently considered we were beginning to run too far ahead of time and the regulator was partially closed, giving only 86½ lb/sq in in the high pressure system, until speed had fallen to 62 when the regulator was opened again, but with the cut-off adjusted so the speed kept around the 60 mark on the undulation to Mars, passed 2½ mins early. The cut-off was further reduced beyond and the speed fell to a sustained 53½ up the three miles at 1 in 200 to St Pierre-le-Moutier. I was somewhat disappointed at the low speed up the bank until I asked the driver what cut-off he was using and learned to my amazement it was only 20 per cent high pressure – a very low figure on a compound, for under these conditions the low pressure cylinders do scarcely any work. It is rare for 241Ps to be driven on less than 30-35 per cent with loads of this magnitude, even on favourable gradients.

The rest of the run to Moulins was taken very easily and in fact the driver overdid things slightly for although Villeneuve was passed in a minute less than the allowance, we ran into Moulins so slowly that a slight loss occurred on the schedule.

The gradients south of Nevers, up the valley of the Allier, tend to be in longer sweeps than those to the north. Between Moulins and St Germain-des-Fosses, the line undulates on easy gradients with nothing worse than two short stretches of 1 in 250 rising for a mile before La Ferte and for 1½ miles just beyond Varennes – and speeds in the upper sixties were maintained on 40/45 per cent cut-offs and less than 200 lb/sq in of steam in the high pressure system. No. 241P8 rode just as well as 241P24 and I was able to make notes quite legibly standing behind the driver. The fireman on 241P8 did not keep pressure up quite as well as his colleague earlier; on 241P24, the stoker had been turning slowly almost continuously when we were in motion. The water on both engines was easily maintained by the pump at between ½ and ¾ of a glass throughout.

The departure from Vichy was 3¾ minutes late with the load by now reduced to 585 tons gross. A gentle start was made to avoid slipping, but once the regulator was opened properly the Mountain responded well. Cut-off was not reduced below 60/65 per cent and the ¾ mile up the 1 in 200 to Pk 368 was mastered at 39mph, while the level mile to the foot of Randan bank at Hauterieve brought speed up to 51. The late start from Vichy had kindled hopes that I might at last be witness to the maximum output of a 241P on the climb to Randan, but the driver was content with 60 per cent hp cut-off and the regulator not quite fully open – how tantalising was the inch of gleaming quadrant visible between the top of the regulator handle and the stop! Speed stabilised at 41 ½mph on the 1 in 91 before falling to a sustained 39 at the tunnel entrance, which marks the summit. A notable effort none the less, particularly in view of the wet rail – for rain and drizzle had followed us all the way from Moret.

Downhill, steam was largely shut off, so as not to exceed the speed restrictions, but once past St Clement hard running was resumed over the undulations to Riom, culminating in a brief maximum of 78½mph down a mile of 1 in 143-200 beyond Ennezat before the driver, now aware of his transgression, slammed on the brake to bring speed within the limit.

At Riom, the driver decided that the tender needed topping up, but the fireman was unable to get the water column to work, the attempt being abandoned and we left 1½ minutes late. There was a slight slipping at the start as the 4-8-2 got hold of her train and the time to Gerzat was not particularly good, though the schedule to Clermont would have been observed were it not for another slow approach and crawl into the platform. The arrival was almost three minutes late – a disappointing end to an excellent run that was otherwise fully representative of day-to-day 241P performance without being in any way exceptional by the standards these remarkable engines set.

Dist		Sched	Actual	Speeds
0.00	MORET-LES-SABLONS	0	0.00	-
5.10	Montigny-sur-Loing		7.43	62/60
7.30	Bourron		9.42	72½/70/73
12.10	NEMOURS-ST-PIERRE	14	13.45	71½
14.85	Bagneaux-sur-Loing		16.02	72½/71
18.70	Souppes		19.14	74/72½
21.50	Dordives		21.31	74/68
25.15	Ferrieres-Fontenay	25	24.37	73/70/74½
29.20	Cepoy		28.02	70
31.65	MONTARGIS	33	32.34	-
7.05	Solterres		9.47	67/64
10.80	Nogent-sur-Vernisson	13	13.11	67/64/68½
15.40	Les Choux-Boismorand		17.19	65/71½
18.80	Pk 148 (Summit)		20.21	65/71½
22.75	GIEN	25	24.51	
6.05	Briare	8	8.10	72½/74½
9.38	Chatillon-sur-Loire	11	10.55	70/74/70
14.00	Bonny-sur-Loire	15	14.50	74
17.35	Neuvy-sur-Loire	18	17.38	70/74½
22.80	Myennes		22.09	70
25.35	COSNE	27	25.21	
5.95	Tracy-Sancerre	9	8.43	70/72½
8.90	Les Girarmes		11.11	71½/66½
11.75	Pouilly-sur-Loire	14	13.42	68½/74
15.40	Mesves-Bulcy		16.48	70/74½/67
19.80	LA CHARITE	22	20.39	62/74½
24.80	Tronsanges		24.56	70/72½
27.95	Pougues-les-Eaux	31	27.41	65
30.30	Garchizy		29.46	73½
32.00	Fourchambault	34	31.09	72½
34.65	Vauzelles		33.29	65/56*
			sigs	18
36.00	NEVERS	40	36.48	
6.55	SANCAIZE	11	10.08	57/71½/60
12.80	Mars	19	16.01	64/62
17.20	ST PIERRE-LE-MOUTER	23	20.27	54/64/54
22.90	Chantenay-St-Imbert	29	26.21	60½/64/60
28.90	Villeneuve-sur-Allier	34	32.04	64/66½

<u>37.30</u>	MOULINS	<u>42</u>	<u>42.22</u>	
8.40	Bessay	11	10.53	70/71½
12.05	La Ferte-Hauterive	14	14.00	68½/70
17.65	Varennes-sur-Allier	19	18.55	66½
21.60	Crecy		22.22	70½
23.60	Billy-Marcenat		24.17	60½
<u>25.70</u>	ST GERMAIN-DES-FOSSES	<u>29</u>	<u>28.46</u>	
				57½/54/59
<u>6.55</u>	VICHY	<u>11</u>	<u>11.39</u>	
1.90	Pk 368		4.37	39
2.80	*Hauterive*	5	5.51	50½
8.60	*Randan Tunnel (summit)*		13.35	39
9.55	Randan	16	14.56	51/64
13.15	St Clement-de-Regnat	20	18.38	60*
15.90	*Thuret*	23	21.06	74½
17.90	*Surat*	25	22.47	68½/71½
20.00	*Ennezat-Clerlande*	27	24.35	70/78½
<u>25.20</u>	RIOM	<u>35</u>	<u>31.14</u>	
4.50	Gerzat		6.35	62/66½
<u>8.50</u>	CLERMONT FERRAND	<u>12</u>	<u>13.18</u>	

* - Speed restriction

INDEX OF
STEAM RUNS

Date	Loco	Journey	Miles	Remarks
Fri 16/02/68	231G97	19:19 Calais M – Amiens	104.50	
Sat 17/02/68	141R17	16:30 Dole V – Besancon V	28.00	
	141R62	18:25 Besancon V – Belfort	60.25	
	141R278	20:30 Belfort – Besancon V	60.25	
Sun 18/02/68	141R912	06:00 Bellegrade – Evian Les Bains	47.75	
	640.145	17:22 Domodossala – Novara	55.75	)
	640.023	19:xx Omegna – Novara	32.25	) On rear
Mon 19/02/68	880.167	08:56 Novara – Sizzano	13.75	
	880.054	13:32 Pavia – Torre Picenardi	59.75	
	880.004	16:59 Torre Picenardi – Cremona	14.25	
	625.123	18:18 Cremona – Olmeneta	6.75	
	625.018	19:37 Olmeneta – Cremona	6.75	
	685.222	20:38 Cremona – Mantova	39.25	
	625.161	22:27 Mantova – Verona	23.00	
Tue 20/02/68	625.156	07:23 Cavazzale – Vicenza	5.00	
	625.034	16:04 Bassano Del Grappo – Padova	29.75	
	625.151	18:26 Venezia Mestre – Maerne-d-M	4.25	) double
	625.039	" " " " " " "		) headed
Wed 21/02/68	93.1422	08:00 Ganserndorf - G Schweinbarth	9.25	) same
	93.1358	09:xx G Schweinbarth - Mistelbach L	13.50	) train
	93.1341	11:22 Mistelbach L - P Rannersdorf	6.75	
	93.1360	12:06 P Rannersdorf - Mistelbach L	6.75	
	93.1358	13:00 Mistelbach - Laa a d Thaya	16.75	
	93.1358	14:10 Laa a d Thaya - Enzersdorf	7.50	
	93.1359	14:32 Enzersdorf - Poysdorf	6.25	
	93.1359	15:10 Poysdorf - Enzersdorf	6.25	

	77.244	15:38 Enzersdorf - Wien Sud	44.75	
	77.281	18:05 Praterstern - Floridsdorf	3.00	
	77.29	18:20 Floridsdorf - Korneuburg	6.75	
Thu 22/02/68	78.617	04:25 Spielfeld Strab - Graz H	29.25	
	52.6689	06:22 Abtissendorf - Puntigam	2.50	
	77.242	07:09 Puntigam - Graz H	3.00	
	78.617	07:37 Graz H - Karlsdorf	8.00	
	52.3364	08:08 Karlsdorf - Graz H	8.00	
	52.3688	12:10 Leoben H - Vordernberg	10.00	) same
	97.209	13:xx Vordernberg - Eisenerz	13.00	) train
	86.781	14:25 Eisenerz - Hieflau	9.25	
	78.624	15:23 Hieflau - Klein Reifling	22.25	
	78.618	16:25 Klein Reifling - Kummerbrucke H	26.00	
	52.2325	17:42 Kummerbrucke H - Hieflau	3.75	) double
	78.601	" " " " " " " "		) headed
	86.642	17:55 Hieflau - Munichtal H	7.50	
	86.782	18:29 Munichtal H - Hieflau	7.50	
	78.619	19:05 Hieflau - Selzthal	23.00	
Fri 23/02/68	77.285	09:40 Seltzthal - Bruck a d Mur	56.50	
	91.40	13:56 Murzzuschlag-Neuberg	6.75	
	91.40	15 40 Neuberg - Murzzuschlag	6.75	
	91.40	16:26 Murzzuschlag - Neuberg	6.75	
	91.40	17:00 Neuberg - Murzzuschlag	6.75	
Sat 24/02/68	241P32	15:53 Langres -Belfort	90.75	) same
	141R244	17:xx Belfort - Delle	14.25	) train
	141R307	18:57 Delle - Belfort	14.25	
	141R569	20:30 Belfort - Besancon V	60.25	
Sun 25/02/68	141TC57	06:17 Paris N - St Denis	3.75	
	141TC64	06:28 St Denis - Paris Nord	3.75	
	141R1294	08:xx Amiens - Boulogne V	76.50	
	231K82	10:43 Boulogne V - Calais V	26.00	
	141R93	14:08 Hazebrouck - Calais M	40.50	
----------------	-----------	--	--------	-----------
Fri 15/03/68	231G81	14:14 Calais M - Amiens	104.50	
	241P7	20:xx Moret Les Sablons - Nevers	115.50	) same
	241P23	21:xx Nevers - Riom	94.50	) train
Sat 16/03/68	241P22	00:00 Riom - Vierzon	143.50	
	141TB463	06:25 Paris Bastille - Boissy St Leger	13.50	
	141TB429	07:50 Boissy St Leger - Paris Bastille	13.50	
	141TB457	09:00 Paris Bastille - Joinville Le Pont	6.25	

	141TB432	09:42 Joinville Le Pont - Paris Reuilly	5.00	
	141TB477	10:04 Paris Reuilly - Joinville Le Pont	5.00	
	141TB457	10:42 Joinville Le Pont - Paris Bastille	6.25	
	241P26	15:xx Chaumont - Belfort	111.00	) same
	141R258	17:xx Belfort - Delle	14.25	) train
	141R444	18:57 Delle - Belfort	14.25	
	141R244	20:30 Belfort - Besancon V	60.25	
Sun 17/03/68	141R1285	08:xx Amiens - Boulogne V	76.50	
	231K31	10:43 Boulogne V - Calais V	26.00	
	141R994	14:08 Hazebrouck - Calais M	40.50	
----------------	------------	---	--------	------------
Sat 18/05/68	03.087	06:13 Monchengladbach H - Herrath	7.50	
	03.252	06:49 Rheydt H - Baal	11.75	
	03.127	07:22 Baal - Monchengladbach H	14.25	
	03.260	08:10 Monchengladbach H - Erkelenz	10.00	
	03.127	09:21 Erkelenz - Herzogenrath	19.25	
	03.077	10:15 Herzogenrath - Monchengladbach H	29.75	
	03.284	11:15 Monchengladbach H - Koln Deutz	36.00	
	03.251	13:06 Koln Deutz - Koln H	0.50	
	01.102	13:53 Koln H - Euskirchen	24.75	
	01.008	15:21 Euskirchen - Koln H	24.75	
	03.276	16:45 Koln H - Monchengladbach H	36.00	
	50.1864	18:07 Monchengladbach H - Kaldenkirchen	16.75	
	03.251	21:55 Rheydt H - Monchengladbach H	2.50	
	03.127	23:05 Monchengladbach H - Aachen H	38.50	
----------------	------------	---	--------	------------
Thu 30/05/68	65.002	06:06 Weinheim B - Furth O	10.50	
	65.002	06:52 Furth O - Weinheim B	10.50	
	038.273-9	09:06 Heidelberg H -Bad Rappenau	30.50	
	038.313-3	10:43 Bad Rappenau - Neckargemund	23.00	
	038.626-8	11:40 Neckargemund - Bad F'hall Jagstfeld	36.75	
	064.017-7	12:56 Bad F'hall Jagstfeld - Heilbronn H	6.75	
	038.626-8	13:51 Heilbronn H - Mannheim H	61.50	
	50.458	16:07 Mannheim H - Heidelberg H	10.50	
	50.2417	17:01 Heidelberg H - Heidelberg Karlstor	2.50	
	038.499-0	17:16 Heidelberg K - Neckargemund	5.00	
	23.076	17:34 Schlierbach Z - Neckargemund	3.00	
	23.086	18:34 Neckargemund - Schlierbach Z	3.00	
	50.2450	18:46 Schlierbach Z - Neckargemund	3.00	
	50.1188	19:00 Neckargemund - Obrigheim	23.00	

	038.313-3	22:28 Neckarelz - Heilbronn H	18.00
Fri 31/05/68	064.017-7	06:01 Heilbronn H - Heilbronn Sulmertor	0.50
	064.235-5	06:17 Heilbronn Sulmertor - Neckarsulm	2.50
	064.018-5	06:31 Neckarsulm - Heilbronn Sulmertor	2.50
	23.076	06:45 Heilbronn Sulmertor - Heilbronn H	0.50
	50.1256	07:27 Heilbronn H - Karlsruhe H	44.75
	038.313-3	09:02 Karlsruhe H - Heilbronn H	44.75	d/headed with DL
	038.626-8	10:20 Heilbronn H - Bad F'hall Jagstfeld	6.75
	050.480-3	10:39 Bad F'hall Jagstfeld - Heilbronn H	6.75
	038.499-0	11:33 Heilbronn H - Crailsheim	54.50
	23.086	13:49 Blaufelden - Crailsheim	13.75
	50.1028	14:30 Crailsheim - Aalen	23.00	) double
	78.355	" " " " " "		) headed
	64.049	16:22 Aalen - Schwabisch Gmund	15.00
	78.300	17:02 Schwabisch Gmund - Schorndorf	13.00
	50.406	17:42 Schorndorf - Pluderhausen	3.00
	78.293	18:24 Pluderhausen - Lorch W	5.00
	50.1638	18:46 Lorch W - Schwabisch Gmund	5.00
	78.355	19:09 Schwabisch Gmund - Lorch W	5.00
	78.298	19:31 Lorch W - Schwabisch Gmund	5.00
	78.297	19:46 Schwabisch Gmund - Schorndorf	13.00
Sat 01/06/68	038.959-3	06:13 Heilbronn H - Bad F Kochendorf	5.50
	23.056	06:34 Bad F Kochendorf - Neckarsulm	2.50
	038.626-8	06:44 Neckarsulm - Bad F'hall Jagstfeld	3.75
	038.273-9	07:16 Bad F'hall Jagstfeld - Heilbronn H	6.75
	44.1559	08:05 Heilbronn H - Waldenburg W	24.25
	23.086	09:34 Waldenburg W - Schwabisch H Hess	13.75
	44.1559	10:08 Schwabisch H Hess - Crailsheim	16.00
	23.105	12:34 Crailsheim - Lauda	43.00
	051.238-4	14:55 Lauda - Konigshofen	1.75
	23.076	15:46 Konigshofen - Osterburken	21.75
	038.959-3	16:57 Osterburken - Bad F'hall Jagstfeld	23.50
	50.227	18:12 Bad F'hall Jagstfeld - Neckarsulm	3.75
	038.711-8	18:30 Neckarsulm - Heilbronn H	3.00
	064.017-7	19:04 Heilbronn H - Schwabisch Hall	33.50
	038.626-8	20:25 Schwabisch Hall - Heilbronn H	33.50	)
	038.313-3	21:31 Heilbronn H - Heidelberg H	51.00	) portion
Sun 02/06/68	23.076	07:13 Neckarelz - Osterburken	18.50
	038.711-8	08:51 Osterburken – Heilbronn H	30.50
	038.313-3	10:16 Heilbronn H - Bad F'hall Jagstfeld	6.75

	038.273-9	10:39 Bad F'hall Jagstfeld - Heilbronn H	6.75	
	038.711-8	11:33 Heilbronn H - Neuenstein	21.25	
	23.072	12:09 Neuenstein - Ohringen	3.75	
	23.019	12:59 Ohringen - Eschenau bH	6.75	
	23.039	13:21 Eschenau bH - Crailsheim	44.75	
	78.482	16:23 Goldshofe - Unterbobingen	13.75	
	78.300	17:29 Unterbobingen - Lorch W	10.50	
	50.864	17:59 Lorch W - Aalen	20.50	
	23.068	19:08 Aalen - Crailsheim	23.00	) same
	038.715-9	19:53 Crailsheim - Schwabisch H Hess	16.00	) train
	23.061	21:05 Schwabisch H Hess - Backnang	26.00	
Mon 03/06/68	038.273-9	06:37 Heilbronn H – Heidelberg Karlstor	40.25	
	50.407	08:16 Heidelberg Karlstor - Heidelberg H	2.50	
	038.273-9	09:06 Heidelberg H - Heilbronn H	42.25	
	038.959-3	11:56 Heilbronn H - Meckesheim	29.25	
	50.227	13:18 Meckesheim - Sinsheim E	6.25	) double-
	038.095-6	" " " " " " " "		) headed
	23.028	16:22 Kaiserslautern - Pirmasens H	22.25	
	23.028	18:50 Pirmasens H - Pirmasens Nord	4.25	
Tue 04/06/68	50.1200	04:09 Saarbrucken H - Hanweiler B R	10.00	) double
	50.3034	" " " " " " " " "		) headed
	50.3034	04:55 Hanweiler B R - Saarbrucken H	10.00	
	01.073	05:31 Saarbrucken H - Wasserbillig	55.50	
----------------	------------	---	--------	------------
Sat 29/06/68	242TA89	07:12 Lille - Tourcoing	8.00	
	242TA102	07:38 Tourcoing - Roubaix	1.75	
	242TA89	0838 Roubaix - Lille	6.25	
	242TA105	10:33 Lille - Roubaix	6.25	
	242TA120	11:xx Roubaix - Tourcoing	1.75	
	242TA102	11:35 Tourcoing - Lille	8.00	
	242TA23	12:47 Lille - Croix Wasquehal	4.25	
	242TA105	13:15 Croix Wasquehal - Lille	4.25	
	141R554	18:xx Corbeil Essonnes - Montargis	57.75	
	241P23	20:14 Montargis - Nevers	83.75	) same
	241P24	21:xx Nevers - St Germain des Fosses	62.75	) train
Sun 30/06/68	141R697	00:50 St Germain des Fosses - Moulins	12.00	
	141R451	02:35 Moulins - Clermont Ferrand	40.50	
	141R1108	06:00 Gannet - St Germain des Fosses	14.25	
	141R650	06:45 St Germain d Fosses - Clerm't F'and	40.50	
----------------	------------	---	--------	------------

Fri 30/08/68	141R587	13:18 Boulogne M - Amiens	76.50
	141R266	18:xx Corbeil Essonnes - Montargis	57.75
	241P24	20:14 Montargis - Nevers	83.75) same
	241P8	21:xx Nevers - St Germain des Fosses	62.75) train
Sat 31/08/68	141R967	01:27 St Germain des Fosses - Moulins	12.00
	241P3	02:22 Moulins - Nevers	49.75) same
	241P22	03:xx Nevers - Moret Les Sablons	115.50) train
	141P150	08:00 Paris Montparnasse - Dreux	51.00
	141P200	09:39 Dreux - Argentan	72.00
	141P115	15:23 Flers Argentan	28.00
	141R68	20:02 Le Mans - Tours	61.50
Sun 01/09/68	241P13	00:18 Le Mans - Angers St Laud	60.25
	141R1303	05:55 Nantes Orleans - Quimper	158.50
	141R1303	19:10 Quimper - Nantes Orleans	158.50
Mon 02/09/68	241P16	00:46 Nantes Orleans - Angers St Laud	5 4.75
	241P32	03:23 Angers St Laud - Nantes Orleans	54.75
	231D648	06:28 Nantes Orleans - Montoir De Bretagne	36.00
	141C181	07:47 Montoir De Bretagne - Savenay	11.75
	231D589	11:14 Le Croisic - Nantes Orleans	57.75) same
	241P30	12:xx Nantes Orleans - Angers St Laud	54.75) train
	241P27	14:xx Angers St Laud - Le Mans	60.25
	141TC37	19:32 Paris Nord - St Denis	3.75
	141TC39	20:10 St Denis - Paris Nord	3.75
Tue 03/09/68	141R618	04:xx Belfort - Montbeliard	11.25
	141R527	06:30 Belfort - Mulhouse	30.50
	141R369	07:44 Mulhouse - Neuenberg	11.75
	50.1858	15:14 Radolfzell - Konstanz	12.50
	50.503	17:22 Radolfzell - Allensbach	5.50
	50.2174	17:48 Allensbach - Singen H	11.75
Wed 04/09/68	50.2668	07:16 Allensbach - Radolfzell	5.50
	38.1282	11:12 Tuttlingen - Rottweil	17.50) same
	38.3369	11:51 Rottweil - Horb	26.75) train
	38.2770	13:04 Horb - Sulz N	8.75
	38.3553	15:19 Sulz N - Rottweil	18.00
	38.2770	16:23 Rottweil - Horb	26.75
	38.2976	17:53 Horb - Tubingen H	20.00
	038.335-6	20:37 Heilbronn H - Wurzburg H	79.00
Thu 05/09/68	050.674-1	05:18 Gemunden M - Schweinfurt H	31.75
	078.303-5	07:07 Poppenhausen - Schweinfurt H	6.25
	01.173	11:26 Lichtenfels - Munchberg	44.00

	01.213	13:26 Munchberg - Hof H	15.00	
	50.745	13:53 Hof H - Oberkotzau	3.75	
	01.169	16:26 Hof H - Marktredwitz	26.00	
	01.111	17:24 Marktredwitz - Holenbrunn	4.25	
	50.1889	18:03 Holenbrunn - Marktredwitz	4.25	
	64.449	18:13 Marktredwitz - Schnabelwaid	30.50	
	64.393	20:07 Bayreuth H - Weiden O	36.00	
Fri 06/09/68	01.059	07:47 Weiden O - Hof H	57.25	
	052.945-3	11:47 Hof H - Falls	25.50	
	01.202	12:51 Falls - Munchberg	10.50	
	01.169	13:24 Munchberg - Kulmbach	25.50	
	01.131	14:12 Kulmbach - Lichtenfels	18.75	
	86.164	16:26 Coburg - Neustadt b C	9.25	
	86.164	16:57 Neustadt b C - Coburg	9.25	
	86.419	17:26 Coburg - Rodach b C	11.25	
	01.213	20:17 Lichtenfels - Neuenmarkt-W	26.00	
Sat 07/09/68	64.449	08:30 Kirchenlaibach - Weiden O	24.25	
	01.173	09:30 Weiden O - Regensburg H	54.00	
	78.482	15:19 Donaworth - Aalen	43.00	
Sun 08/09/68	03.222	Eurovapour Rail Tour	108.00	
	03.281	19:35 Friedrichshafen - Ulm H	64.50	
----------------	------------	--	--------	------------
Sat 19/10/68	141R985	09:56 Hazebrouk - Calais V	38.50	
	231K27	11:23 Calais V - Calais M	2.00	
	231K8	14:14 Calais M - Boulogne V	28.00	
	231K22	16:00 Boulogne V - Rang Du Fliers	23.50	
	141R1285	17:03 Rang Du Fliers - Boulogne V	23.50	
	141R500	18:38 Boulogne V - Calais V	26.00	
	141R508	20:10 Calais V - Hazebrouk	38.50	
----------------	------------	--	--------	------------
Fri 08/11/68	141TC34	09:01 Paris Nord - Ermont Eaubonne	8.75	
	141TC30	09:43 Ermont Eaubonne - Argenteuil	3.00	
	141TC30	09:43 Argenteuil - Ermont Eaubonne	3.00	
	141TC37	10:13 Ermont Eaubonne - Enghien L B	1.75	
	141TC40	10:44 Enghien L B - Epinay Villetaneuse	1.25	
	141TC57	10:54 Epinay Villetaneuse - Paris Nord	6.00	
	141TC15	13:30 Paris Nord - St Denis	3.75	
	141TC24	13:42 St Denis - Persan Beaumont	18.75	
	141TC31	15:08 Persan Beaumont - E'nt Eaubonne	15.00	
	141TC28	16:07 Ermont Eaubonne - St Denis	5.00	

	141TC13	16:37 St Denis - Paris Nord	3.75	
	241P16	19:xx Le Mans - Sable	30.50	
	241P13	20:52 Sable - Nantes Orleans	84.50	
Sat 09/11/68	141TB500	09:00 Paris Bastille - Joinville Le Pont	6.25	
	141TB429	09:43 Joinville Le Pont - Paris Bel Air	4.25	
	141TB461	10:06 Paris Bel Air - Boissy St Leger	11.75	
	141TB461	11:17 Boissy St Leger - Paris Bastille	13.50	
	141TC12	12:35 Paris Nord St Denis	3.75	
	141TC5	12:54 St Denis - Ermont Eaubonne	5.00	
	141TC34	13:18 Ermont Eaubonne - Paris Nord	10.50	
	141R1294	16:xx Amiens - Boulogne V	76.50	
	141R93	18:38 Boulogne V - Calais V	26.00	
	141R189	20:10 Calais V - Hazebrouck	38.50	
Sat 07/12/68	141R1285	08:05 Calais V - Etaples	43.00	
	141R1201	09:52 Etaples - Boulogne V	16.75	
	231K8	10:43 BoulogneV - Calais V	26.00	
	141R1219	14:06 Hazebrouck - Calais V	38.50	
	231K8	15:10 Calais V - Rang Du Fliers	49.75	
	141R1285	17:03 Rang Du Fliers – Calais V	49.75	
	141R1294	19:02 Calais V - Frethun Les Calais	5.00	
	141R476	19:21 Frethun Les Calais - Calais V	5.00	
	141R1219	20:10 Calais V - Hazebrouck	38.50	
Sat 11/01/69	141TC7	09:01 Paris Nord - Ermont Eaubonne	8.75	
	141TC59	09:30 Ermont Eaubonne - Pontoise	9.50	
	141TC59	10:40 Pontoise - Paris Nord	18.75	
	231K82	13:xx Amiens - Calais M	104.50	
Fri 21/02/69	880.038	13:51 Cavallermaggiore - Bra	8.00	) same
	640.121	14:xx Bra - Alessandria	52.75	) train
	640.019	18:18 Casale Monferrato - Valenza	11.75	
	640.121	19:09 Valenza - Pavia	31.75	
Sat 22/02/69	640.019	03:58 Alessandria - Vercelli	34.75	
	640.019	05:52 Vercelli - Pavia	41.75	
	625.157	14:38 Milano Porto Garibaldi - Treviglio	20.50	
	625.149	18:22 Brescia - Olmeneta	24.75	
	880.058	21:42 Cava Tigozzi - Cremona	2.50	
Sun 23/02/69	685.215	07:05 Cremona - Treviglio	40.50	
	625.129	11:15 Brescia - Calolziocorte Olginate	47.25	

	685.222	13:50 Calolziocorte Olginate - Brescia	47.25	
Mon 24/02/68	06.218	06:29 Zidani Most - Zagreb G K	52.75	
	11.059	15:22 Sid - Stara Pazova	51.00	
	01.097	21:00 Stara Pazova - Beograd	21.75	
	38.066	23:00 Beograd - Lapovo	68.25	) double
	05.011	" " " " " "		) headed
Tue 25/02/69	05.011	02:xx Lapovo - Nis	83.25	) same
	05.004	06:xx Nis - Vladicin Han	53.50	) train
	05.013	10:33 Vladicin Han - Nis	53.50	) same
	05.025	14:xx Nis - Beograd	151.50	) train
Wed 26/02/69	06.021	08:00 Zagreb G K - Maribor	118.00	
	06.006	14:32 Maribor - Spielfeld Strab	13.50	
	52.7070	16:40 Spielfeld Strab - Leibnitz	6.75	
	52.7570	17:03 Leibnitz - Graz H	22.25	
	52.7070	18:48 Graz H - Werndorf	11.00	
	52.7012	19:32 Werndorf - Graz H	11.00	
Thu 27/02/69	52.1098	04:32 Wiener Neustadt - Wampersdorf	13.00	
	77.261	05:30 Wampersdorf - Wien Sud	21.75	
	93.1333	07:58 Stammersdorf - Hohenau	56.00	
	93.1333	11:05 Hohenau - Mistelbach L	17.50	
	93.1397	14:00 Mistelbach L - Grob Schweinbarth	13.50	
	93.1425	15:26 Grob Schweinbarth - Pirawarth	3.00	
	93.1378	15:47 Pirawarth - Grob Schweinbarth	3.00	) double-
	93.1334	" " " " " " " "		) headed
	93.1397	15:56 Grob Schweinbarth - Ganserndorf	9.25	
	77.11	17:04 Florisdorf - Bernhardsthal	43.50	
Fri 28/02/69	78.613	06:08 Amstetten - Klein Reifling	28.00	
	78.609	09:40 Klein Reifling - Amstetten	28.00	
	52.7017	17:05 Linz H - Gaisbach Wartberg	16.75	
Sat 01/03/69	50.2838	13:16 Waldshut - Basle Bad H	34.25	
	141R375	18:41 Strasbourg - Saarbrucken H	71.50	
	23.077	21:19 Saarbrucken H - Saarbrucken B	1.75	
	23.030	21:33 Saarbrucken B - Saarbrucken H	1.75	
	50.2886	22:18 Saarbrucken H - Luisenthal S	3.75	
Sun 02/03/69	141R116	14:06 Hazebrouck - Calais M	40.50	
----------------	------------	--	--------	------------
Sat 29/03/69	141TC43	09:01 Paris Nord - Ermont Eaubonne	8.75	
	141TC12	09:28 Ermont Eaubonne - Sannois	1.25	
	141TC20	10:01 Sannois - Ermont Eaubonne	1.25	
	141TC62	10:13 Ermont Eaubonne - Champ CDE	1.25	

	141TC47	10:41 Champ CDE - Epinay Villetaneuse	1.75	
	141TC48	10:54 Epinay Villetaneuse - St Denis	1.75	
	141TC6	11:13 St Denis - Epinay Villetaneuse	1.75	
	141TC40	11:24 Epinay Villetaneuse - Champ CDE	1.75	
	141TC10	11:42 Champ CDE - Le Barre O	1.25	
	141TC50	12:02 Le Barre O - Enghien L B	0.50	
	141TC41	12:18 Enghien L B - Ermont Eaubonne	1.75	
	141TC17	13:25 Ermont Eaubonne - Champ CDE	1.25	
	141TC3	13:58 Champ CDE - Paris Nord	7.50	
	141R502	15:xx Amiens - Calais V	102.50	
	141R314	19:02 Calais V - Frethun Les Calais	5.00	
	141R148	19:21 Frethun Les Calais - Calais V	5.00	
	141R338	20:10 Calais V - Hazebrouck	38.50	
Sat 27/09/69	141R93	15:xx Amiens - Calais V	102.50	
	141R1215	19:02 Calais V - Les Fontinettes	1.75	
	141R189	19:xx Les Fontinettes - Calais V	1.75	
	141R497	20:10 Calais V - Hazebrouck	38.50	
Sun 03/05/70	141R180	Xx:xx Amiens - Calais M	104.50	
Wed 20/05/70	141R994	Xx:xx Calais M - Amiens	104.50	
Sat 12/09/70	141R542	Xx:xx Boulogne M - Amiens	76.50	
Mon 05/10/70	03.2081-2	Xx:xx Berlin Zoo - Helmstedt	116.25	

SOUTHERN-Images

the home of quality archive photos

PO Box 218
ALTON
Hants
GU34 9AA
http://www.southern-images.co.uk/

Welcome to SOUTHERN-Images, the online archive which provides a fully searchable source of high quality photographs. We own well over 50,000 original slides and negatives arranged in twelve Collections and also host images from a number of well known photographers. Our subject matter is primarily the railways of Britain, but we also have a growing collection of photos of other forms of transport and general interest. Our oldest train photo is from 1908, and we have steam trains, diesel and electric trains right up to the present day. You can order photos for sale online by credit card or you can obtain repro rights for editoral and commercial use.

Featured Photographers and Collections:

John H. Bird

C. H. Gooch

Keith Lawrence

Anthony Ward Collection

Keith Widdowson

Frequently asked questions.

What sort of photos do you have available?
We have over 50,000 original colour and black/white negatives and slides, dating back to 1903. Our specialism is train and railway photos of Britain during the 20th century. We also have a growing collection of photos of road transport, ships and aircraft, as well as places, buildings, flora, fauna and wildlife, especially from Southern England. New photos are added every week.

I am interested in buying a photograph from SOUTHERN-Images. How much will it cost?
You can buy a 6" x 4" print for less than £1,or at the other end of the scale enlargements up to 30" x 20"! There are many other sizes available in between and these are all listed beside each photograph on the website. These prices apply to photos bought for personal purposes only-such photos are copyright and may not be reproduced or published in any way.

I want to use a photograph from SOUTHERN-Images in a newspaper/ magazine/book/etc. How do I go about it? What will it cost?
Our photos have been used in UK national newspapers, magazines, record sleeves, advertisements and so on. You can obtain limited reproduction rights instantly online: for other uses email us for a quotation. Our rates for non-exclusive use of photos are quite modest compared to most other photo archives. Rates are negotiable and this will be especially attractive to charities and small-scale low-budget publishers/editors. Photos can be e-mailed to you as high resolution jpgs or mailed on CD/DVD, or as photographic prints.

I would like to download one of your photos for personal use on my website.
You can buy a digital image of any photo in the archive and it will be sent to you as an e-mail attachment (approximately 600 pixels wide) without any copyright branding, provided it is for private use only.

I want to buy photos but I don't want to use a credit card online.
That's no problem, although credit card orders are very secure and ensure quickest delivery of your order. However, you can easily download an order form from this site and pay by cheque as a mail order.